Pearson Education

AP* Test Prep Series

AP HUMAN GEOGRAPHY

To accompany:

The Cultural Landscape:
An Introduction to Human Geography

AP* Edition, 10e, ©2011

JAMES M. RUBENSTEIN

JOHN PHILIP ANTONY HURT

Social Studies Department Chair, Heritage High School, Littleton, CO

SHANNA L. HURT

Social Studies Department, Arapahoe High School, Littleton, CO

Prentice Hall

Boston Columbus Indianapolis New York San Francisco Upper Saddle River
Amsterdam Cape Town Dubai London Madrid Milan Munich Paris Montréal Toronto
Delhi Mexico City São Paulo Sydney Hong Kong Seoul Singapore Taipei Tokyo

Geography Editor: Christian Botting
Marketing Manager: Maureen McLaughlin
Managing Editor, Geosciences and Chemistry: Gina M. Cheselka
Project Manager: Ed Thomas
Supplement Cover Designer: Paul Gourhan
Operations Supervisor: Maura Zaldivar
Cover Photo Credit: epa/Corbis

Pearson Education AP* Test Prep Series for
The Cultural Landscape: An Introduction to Human Geography, AP* Edition

© 2011, 2008, 2005
Pearson Education, Inc.
Pearson Prentice Hall
Upper Saddle River, NJ 07458

* Advanced Placement, Advanced Placement Program, AP, and Pre-AP are registered trademarks of The College Board, which was not involved in the production of, and does not endorse, these products.

Printed in the United States of America

10   9   8   7   6   5

ISBN-13:   978-0-13-137556-7
ISBN-10:   0-13-137556-3

Prentice Hall
is an imprint of

Please visit our Web site at http://www.PearsonSchool.com/Advanced

Table of Contents

Introduction to Advanced Placement Human Geography:

Advanced Placement Human Geography is an introductory college course in human geography. The exam assumes that you have taken the equivalent of one semester of college-level preparation, with the understanding that many high schools will teach the course for one year, depending on their schedules.

All material on the exam has been selected by geographers who are members of the AP Human Geography Development Committee. The material included in this guide correlates to what they feel is a typical introductory college course in human geography. The exam at the end of the school year is representative of this material and is considered an appropriate measure of skills and knowledge needed in the field of introductory human geography.

The prescribed curriculum for this course is outlined by The College Board, and it gives you a learning experience similar to what you would obtain in a college level introductory human geography course. It is at the discretion of the school to develop the course to work into their already existing schedule.

The purpose of this course is to introduce you to the systematic study of patterns and processes that have shaped human understanding, use and alteration of Earth's surface. As a geography student, you will look spatially at the Earth to analyze humans' organization of space and the environmental consequences of their decisions. You will be looking for patterns across the cultural landscape, trying to identify trends and then anticipate future phenomena that might occur across the landscape. You will also explore different methods and tools geographers use in their science and practice.

Goals of Advanced Placement Human Geography:

AP Human Geography was established with five college-level goals in mind. These goals are aligned directly with the National Geography Standards that were developed in 1994. Upon successful completion of the course, you should have developed geographic skills that enable you to:

Use and think about maps and spatial data.
Maps and spatial data are essential in discovering patterns on the Earth's surface that reflect and influence physical and human processes. Learning to use and think critically with these tools will allow you to use real world data to problem solve various situations on Earth. Thinking critically about what is obvious and also that which is hidden on various maps gives you the understanding you need to successfully use maps and spatial data.

Understand and interpret the implications of associations among phenomena in places.
Geographers look at data and map sets in order to understand changes in the spatial organization of the Earth's surface. They are particularly interested in focusing on how phenomena (*an observable fact, occurrence or circumstance*) are related to one another

in particular places. You should be able to not only recognize and interpret patterns, but also to identify the nature and significance of the relationships among phenomena that occur in the same place. In addition, you should understand how a culture's values and tastes, political situations, and economic conditions help to create unique cultural landscapes.

Recognize and interpret at different scales the relationships among patterns and processes.
Geographic study also requires that you view patterns at different scales. Geography really is a matter of scale. You should understand that a phenomena looked at on a local scale could very well be influenced by circumstances occurring at another scale - national, local, or even global. You should look for the connections operating at multiple scales when trying to explain geographic patterns and arrangements.

Define regions and evaluate the regionalization process.
Geography is not only concerned with identifying patterns across the cultural landscape, but also with analyzing how they came about and what they mean. In order to successfully make such an analysis, you need to break the patterns into smaller parts or categories, referred to as regions. By looking critically at regions of the world, you will be able to consider how and why the regions emerged and hypothesize the implications for future development of the Earth's surface.

Characterize and analyze changing interconnections among places.
In order to obtain the true depth of the geographic perspective, you must understand that events and processes occurring in one place can have a profound influence on other places. You should look at places and patterns as part of a whole, not in isolation. Be aware that relationships on Earth are in constant motion, they are continually changing, and your job is to figure out how and why this change occurs.

Topics in Advanced Placement Human Geography:

I. Geography: Its Nature and Perspectives
This course emphasizes geography as a field of academic study and gives a brief overview of geography in nineteenth-century Europe. This overview will show how the discipline has evolved into the study of diverse cultures and unique areas organized around some key concepts.

You will be introduced to the importance of spatial organization - the location of places, people and events on Earth. In addition you will look for the global connections of places and landscapes in order to understand human activity across the Earth's surface.

Key concepts that will be important throughout the course are location, space, place, scale, pattern, regionalization and globalization. These concepts are essential for your understanding of spatial interaction and spatial organization of the Earth's surface. You should be able to successfully analyze human population growth and movement, cultural patterns, economic use of the Earth, political organization of space, and human settlement patterns, especially urbanization. You will learn how to use and interpret maps in order to make these analyses. The course will allow you to apply mathematical formulas, models and qualitative date to these geographic concepts in order to make educated predictions. The course will also ask that you make regional analysis of various phenomena and create appropriate regions to illustrate certain processes.

Ultimately, this course should allow you to see the relevance of academic geography in everyday life and decision making. You should be able to apply these key concepts when looking at current events and policies. You should be able to ask yourself the following questions: "If I were a policy maker for the United Nations, why would this information be important? How would I use it to develop public policy that would impact humans in sub-Saharan Africa, Europe, and North America?"

II: Population

An important geographic concept is how populations are organized over the Earth's surface. This part of the course gives you the tools you need to make sense of cultural, political, economic and urban systems. By analyzing demographic data such as infant mortality rates, crude death rates, crude birth rates, and migration, you will understand the distribution of human population at different scales: global, continental, national, state and local community. You will be able to explain why populations are growing or declining in certain places and not others. You will be asked to discover where and why fertility rates have dropped in some parts of the developing world, but not in others. Look at how age-sex structures (population pyramids) are different in many regions of the world and explain the political, cultural, economic implications of these differences. A key component of population geography that is important in today's world is your understanding of refugee flows, immigration (both internal and out-migration) and residential mobility (movement to the Sunbelt) in order to appreciate the interconnectedness of our world. The relationship between refugees and political boundaries is also important, especially where refugees have no access to political power because they find themselves "on the wrong side of the line." Another key concept related to populations is that of environmental degradation. With increases in regional populations, many stresses occur on the environment, thus causing rapid out-migration and urbanization. Rapid immigration to certain parts of the world can exacerbate anti-foreigner sentiment because of the imbalance that occurs in wages, employment and political power. You will also compare different models of population change, including demographic and epidemiological transitions, and government population policies. Upon completion of this unit, you should be able to evaluate the role, strengths and weaknesses of major population policies and make recommendations regarding them. For instance, is education essential in lowering fertility rates? Should females be empowered in order to accomplish this?

III. Cultural Patterns and Processes

Critical to your understanding of human geography is your ability to analyze and predict various components of regional cultural patterns and processes. In order to be successful in doing this you will be learning about the concept of culture. What is culture? What makes up a person's culture? We begin by looking at the spatial distribution of cultural groups as defined by their language, religion, race, ethnicity and gender. It is vital to look at the past and the present in your analysis, as the spatial distribution of these characteristics changes over time.

You must look at cultural patterns from a variety of geographic scales, starting with local and then moving to the global scale. Diffusion is a key concept when you are looking at these patterns. For example, you might look at the location of certain agricultural processes, or housing types, or where certain religions or languages are practiced. How did these traits get from point A to point B? Your job is to analyze these patterns of diffusion.

In this analysis the concept of folk culture versus popular culture will emerge. This is an important way to differentiate between cultures. Folk cultures tend to be isolated and will only diffuse through relocation, like the Amish culture. Popular cultures are global and relocate through many different types of diffusion. You will be able to distinguish between the languages and dialects, religious practices, ethnic and universalizing religions, as well as the popular or folk culture of a group. This will lead to your understanding of geographic patterns. You will see that each culture leaves a unique imprint on the landscape.

One important aspect of this section of the course is to look at the way culture shapes human-environmental relationships. The root word for culture is *cultus (to care for)*, so when making your analysis of what a cultural group cares about, look around. If someone visits a major city in the USA, what would they see - NFL football stadiums, NBA stadiums, NBL fields? This cultural landscape reflects what people in that culture do with their spare time and money. Would the landscape look the same in different regions, like the Middle East or Europe? Landscapes tend to reflect the cultural values, tastes and sets of beliefs of a group of people. By looking at these landscapes you should be able to identify cultural traits, like the language and religion of a group of people. This will help you to build a cultural map of the group. Where did they begin, where did they move to, where are they now, where will they be in the future?

IV. Political Organization of Space
This section of the course will introduce you to the political organization of the Earth's surface at a variety of scales. You need to keep in mind that the political boundaries that have been drawn over the years reflect somebody's view of how the earth should be divided. This view is sometimes in conflict with other's views of where a boundary should be and thus problems can occur.

The main emphasis is on the concept of a "nation-state" or country. How did the current world map emerge? What political entities were at play to get the boundaries we have today? You will be looking at the world in historic terms, so that you might be able to analyze these changes over time. For example, you should be able to see the impact of colonialism on these boundaries, as well as the devolution of the former Soviet Union. You will notice that often there is no correlation between ethnic, economic or environmental patterns and the contemporary world map. You will consider forces that are changing the role of individual nation-states in the contemporary world, like ethnic conflicts, supranationalism, economic globalization, regional economic blocs and the need to confront environmental issues that know no political boundaries.

In order to truly understand the complexities associated with political boundaries, you must look at the issues at different scales, such as political units above and below the state. Political units above the state level would be regional alliances, such as NATO, the European Union or the United Nations. If you wanted to look at the scale below the state, then you would be analyzing entities like city boundaries, ethnic boundaries, and voting districts. In addition, you will study how specific policies affect the spatial organization of cultural and social life, such as racial segregation.

V. Agricultural and Rural Land Use
In this portion of the course you will explore four basic themes: the origin and diffusion of agriculture, key characteristics of the world's agricultural regions, reasons why these regions function the way they do, and the environmental impact of agriculture. First it is important to examine where domesticated agricultural practices began and look at the diffusion of these practices around the globe. You will understand the impacts of diet, energy use, and new technologies on the emergence of sedentary societies.

Next you will look at the Earth's major agricultural production regions. You will examine both extensive activity (fishing, forestry, nomadic herding, ranching, and shifting cultivation), and intensive activity (plantation agriculture, mixed crop/livestock systems, market gardening, factory farms, and horticulture). You will also be concerned with land survey systems, environmental conditions, and cultural values that create and sustain these patterns.

One theory that will be important to your understanding of explanations for the location of agricultural activities is Von Thunen's agricultural land use model. Other agricultural activities such as the impact of factory farming on food supplies, and the distribution of crops and animals are also emphasized. The need to increase food production concludes your study of agriculture. What will be the impact of genetically modified crops (biotechnology) on food production?

VI. Industrialization and Economic Development
Economic activity can be analyzed by looking at the interaction of natural resources, culture, politics and history in specific places. It is this interaction that allows you to get a spatial perspective of areas across our cultural landscape. By looking at these key concepts (natural resources, culture, politics, history), you will be able to appreciate why resources have different values in different societies around the globe. These values give regions comparative advantages for development over other regions.

Economic development models will be studied throughout this unit. You will look at Rostow's stages of economic growth, where he argued that countries will go through five stages of development beginning with traditional societies and ending with a nation characterized by high mass consumption. By looking at Immanuel Wallerstein's World Systems Theory (core-periphery), you will be able to explain why the world has emerged into a well-developed core and a less-developed periphery. During this time you will compare location theories, such as Weber and von Thunen, in order to understand if these theories are still valid in our ever globalizing world. Does time-space compression still hold true? Why have Asian markets flourished, while sub-Saharan markets have declined? What is the impact of economic growth on North America? Why is that region in decline?

You will also be looking at contemporary issues that surround economic activity. By looking at these issues at various scales, you will see how new patterns of economic inequity emerge. How will certain communities or countries deal with pollution and the quality of life? What will be the impact of deindustrialization, the disaggregation of production, and the rise of consumption and leisure activities on the community, the country, and the region?

VII. Cities and Urban Land Use

The urban geography unit focuses on the development and character of cities, and the internal structure and landscape of urban areas. In order to appreciate the study of cities, you will look at historical and current locations of cities, as well as their political, economic and cultural functions. You will also analyze transportation and communications among cities, and begin to understand why there are differences in the growth of cities. Many of these differences will be tied to their political, economic or cultural traits. Theories that will be examined during this first part of the unit will be Christaller's central place theory, the rank size rule, and the gravity model. Quantitative information, such as demographic data, migration, zones of influence, or the effects of job creation programs are used to analyze changes in the urban hierarchy.

The second focus will be on the internal structure and landscapes of urban areas. You will be evaluating what it would be like to live and work in a large city. You will be looking at land use patterns, racial and ethnic segregation, transportation systems within the city, architecture patterns, and cycles of development. Within this study, you will continue to use qualitative data from the census bureau, as well as qualitative information that you will collect from narrative accounts and field studies. You will be presented with different models of internal city structure: the Burgess concentric zone model, the Hoyt sector model, and the Harris-Ullman multiple nuclei model. (*Note: sometimes on the AP Exam, these models might only be called by the model name, like sector model, instead of Hoyt sector model*) When studying these models it is important for you to look at the architectural history and emergence of transportation within the city to truly appreciate the city's cultural landscape.

You will study new trends in urban development, such as the emergence of edge cities and the gentrification of neighborhoods. You will be looking at new types of urban planning initiatives and community actions that help shape the future of cities.

Although most urban geographers focus on North American cities, it will be important for you to compare urban structures in other parts of the world. The study of European, Islamic, East and South Asian, Latin American, and sub-Saharan African cities can illustrate the cultural values and economic systems of different regions. This will help you to see the spatial distribution and patterns that have been prevalent throughout this course.

The AP Exam

The AP Human Geography exam is about 2 hours and 15 minutes in length and includes both a 60-minute multiple-choice section and a 75-minute free-response section. Each section accounts for half of the student's exam grade.

The following are the approximate percentages of the multiple-choice section that are devoted to each area:

I. Geography: Its Nature and Perspectives	5-10%
II. Population	13-17%
III. Cultural Patterns and Processes	13-17%
IV. Political Organization of Space	13-17%
V. Agriculture and Rural Land Use	13-17%
VI. Industrialization and Economic Development	13-17%
VII. Cities and Urban Land Use	13-17%

Your exam score is converted into The College Board AP Central's 5-point scale as follows:

5	Extremely well qualified
4	Well qualified
3	Qualified
2	Possibly qualified
1	No recommendation

Strategies for Success in Advanced Placement Human Geography

1. Thinking geographically

Much of the content of this course deals with themes and issues that are integral to our world today. For example, population policies, political conflicts between and within countries, and the problems of suburban sprawl are all regular newsworthy items. The key is to think about current events in geographical terms. Students should always consider the spatial aspects of world events. For example, in a conflict between two countries, the geographical importance lies in understanding boundary disputes, the location of different ethnic groups, conflict over land and resources, and infrastructural considerations. This way of thinking should be imprinted throughout the course.

2. Using and interpreting graphs, maps, and charts

The textbook contains numerous graphics, especially maps. It is critical that students practice reading and interpreting these maps. Make sure that they understand the title, key, and scale, and can describe what the map is showing. Specific graphics must be understood. For example, what does a population pyramid show? There will be graphs, maps, and charts on the Advanced Placement Human Geography examination, both in the multiple-choice section and the free-response questions. This guide includes activities and free-response questions that integrate graphs, maps, and charts so that students can practice reading and interpreting them.

3. Integrating the content

In the high school Social Studies curriculum, we tend to think in compartments such as history, geography, economics, and politics. Within this course, we do the same thing, and consider topics such as political geography, industry and development, and urbanization. It is imperative that students have a more holistic way of thinking before they go into the examination. For example, ethnicity and political geography overlap. Population is relevant to urbanization, and development incorporates material from other units in the course. Some of the free-response questions on the examination will require students to draw information from a number of different units, and so they must integrate the content.

4. Knowledge and use of case studies

In both sections of the examination, students will be required to answer questions that involve a specific knowledge and understanding of different places in the world. On the free-response section they may have to exemplify a concept with a specific example. Thus a working knowledge of case studies is essential. These may include the Middle East, the Balkans and the breakup of Yugoslavia, ethnic and political conflict in the Caucasus, or the political boundaries of Africa. In each of the above case studies, there are geographic issues that transcend specific chapters in the text. For example, students should be familiar with population, religious, ethnic, political, and economic aspects of regional case studies as appropriate.

5. A broad geographical knowledge

More than any other geography course, Advanced Placement Human Geography requires students to think and write critically in the content area. This should not take away from the fact that they also need to have a working knowledge of world political geography. For example, they should be expected to have a pretty good idea of which countries colonized different parts of the developing world, and the characteristics of different regions of the globe. Can students identify the major countries in each region or realm of the world? In the context of higher level questions, the examination will still require this knowledge. For example, a map that accompanies a free-response question will often show political boundaries without showing the names of countries, and students will be expected to identify these countries correctly.

6. Knowledge and use of models

Models are integral to human geography, and students need to be familiar with them. These include but are not limited to the demographic and migration transition, models of industrial location and agricultural land use, development models, central place theory, and models of urban structure. Students should know the title, content, and author of the model together with the underlying assumptions. Where they deviate from reality, students need to be able to explain those differences. To what extent is the model useful in explaining spatial reality in that context? Students' knowledge of models in human geography will be tested on the examination. It is always possible that one of the free-response questions will focus on a specific model.

7. Material from a variety of texts and other support materials

This textbook covers most of the key concepts and content areas of the course. The correlation guide aligns every part of the Advanced Placement Human Geography outline to key issues throughout the text. The key vocabulary terms are highlighted and defined in the textbook, and highlighted again in this guide. Together they provide the necessary content for success in the course. At the same time it must be realized that the examiners are not working from this text alone. Thus it is the instructor's responsibility to make sure that students are exposed to some other materials and texts as part of the preparation for the examination. This guide has made every effort to contain a review of all the content and vocabulary that might be part of the Advanced Placement Human Geography examination, including material that is only briefly mentioned or not covered in Rubenstein's text.

8. Review and exam preparation

This guide is a comprehensive review and examination preparation manual. Students need to take the practice tests under exam conditions. The guide includes two multiple-choice examinations of 75 questions each, together with six free-response questions. On the multiple-choice section they need to read the entire question and use a process of elimination. If they can narrow it down to two choices and make an educated guess, then they should answer it, but if they are completely unsure of an answer, they should leave it blank. Students lose .25 points for each wrong answer.

On the free-response questions students should read the question, underlining key terms, and then spend a few minutes jotting down ideas and making an outline that will help them to answer it. If a question is organized A, B, and C, make sure their answer follows the same format. Introductory and concluding paragraphs are not necessary; students should get to the point quickly and be as succinct as possible. Recognize what the question is asking. One that asks a student to evaluate or analyze involves more, and will be worth more points than one where the task is to list or describe. Use specific examples where asked to do so. There are three free-response questions on the exam, each of which must be answered (unlike some Advanced Placement examinations there is no choice). Some questions will deal with content material specific to one unit while others will require students to draw upon material from more than one unit.

On both sections of the examination they should be cognizant of the time limit throughout. On the multiple-choice part of the exam, students should come back to questions where they are unsure. Even though they lose .25 points for each wrong answer, they shouldn't leave many blank. On the free-response questions, students should answer the question(s) about which they are most confident first, leaving what they consider to be the most difficult to last. It is imperative that they try to answer all the questions. Unlike the multiple-choice part of the test, students do not lose points for wrong answers.

Correlation Guide for the Advanced Placement Human Geography Units and <u>The Cultural Landscape: An Introduction to Human Geography, AP* Edition 10e textbook.</u>

Listed below are the seven units for AP Human Geography as they correlate to the key issues in each chapter of the textbook:

AP Outline	Textbook Chapters and Key Issues
Unit 1: Geography: Its Nature and Perspectives	
A. Geography as a field of inquiry	Chapter 1 Key Issue 1
B. Geographical concepts and models	Chapter 1 Key Issue 1
C. Key concepts underlying the geographical perspective	Chapter 1 Key Issues 1, 2, and 3
D. Key Geographical skills:	
1) Maps and spatial data	Chapter 1 Key Issue 1
2) Implications of associations among phenomena in places	Chapter 1 Key Issue 2
3) Different scales and relationships among patterns	Chapter 1 Key Issue 3
4) Regions and the regionalization processes	Chapter 1 Key Issue 2
5) Changing interconnections among places	Chapter 1 Key Issue 3
E. Geographic Technologies	Chapter 1 Key Issue 1
F. Sources of geographical ideas and data	Chapter 1 Key Issue 1
Unit 2: Population	
A. Geographical analysis of population	
1) Density, distribution, and scale	Chapter 2 Key Issue 1
2) Consequences of various densities and distributions	Chapter 2 Key Issue 1
3) Patterns of composition: age, sex, race, ethnicity	Chapter 2 Key Issue 3
4) Population and natural hazards	Chapter 3 Key Issue 1
B. Population growth and decline over time and space	
1) Historical trends and projections	Chapter 2 Key Issues 2 and 4
2) Theories of population growth	Chapter 2 Key Issue 2
3) Patterns of fertility, mortality and health	Chapter 2 Key Issues 2 and 4
4) Regional variations of demographic transitions	Chapter 2 Key Issue 3
5) Effects of population policies	Chapter 2 Key Issue 4; Chapter 3 Key Issue 3
C. Population Movement	
1) Migration selectivity	Chapter 3 Key Issue 2
2) Major voluntary and involuntary migrations	Chapter 3 Key Issues 1, 2, and 4
3) Theories of migration	Chapter 3 Key Issue 1
4) International migration and refugees	Chapter 3 Key Issue 1
5) Socioeconomic consequences of migration	Chapter 3 Key Issues 1, 2, 3, and 4
Unit 3: Cultural Patterns and Processes	
A. Concepts of culture	
1) Traits	Chapter 4 Key Issue 1; Chapter 5 Key Issues 1, 2, and 3; Chapter 6 Key Issue 1; Chapter 7 Key Issues 1 and 2
2) Diffusion	Chapter 1 Key Issue 4; Chapter 4 Key Issues 1 and 3; Chapter 5 Key Issue 1; Chapter 6 Key Issue 2; Chapter 7 Key Issue 1
3) Acculturation	Chapter 5 Key Issue 4; Chapter 6 Key Issue 2
4) Cultural regions	Chapter 5 Key Issues 1, 2, and 3; Chapter 6 Key Issues 1, 2 and 3; Chapter 7 Key Issue 2
B. Cultural Differences	
1) Language	Chapter 5 Key Issues 1, 2, 3, and 4
2) Religion	Chapter 6 Key Issues 1, 2, 3, and 4

3) Ethnicity	Chapter 6 Key Issue 4; Chapter 7 Key Issues 1, 2, 3, and 4
4) Gender	Chapter 4 Key Issue 4
5) Popular and folk culture	Chapter 4 Key Issues 1, 2, 3, and 4
C. Cultural landscapes and cultural identity	
1) Values and preferences	Chapter 4 Key Issues 2 and 4; Chapter 5 Key Issue 4; Chapter 6 Key Issues 2 and 3
2) Symbolic landscapes and sense of place	Chapter 4 Key Issue 2; Chapter 5 Key Issue 4; Chapter 6 Key Issues 2 and 3
3) Environmental impact of cultural attitudes and practices	Chapter 4 Key Issues 2 and 4; Chapter 6 Key Issue 3
Unit 4: Political Organization of Space	
A. Territorial dimensions of politics	
1) Concept of territoriality	Chapter 8 Key Issue 1
2) Nature and meaning of boundaries	Chapter 8 Key Issue 2
3) Influences of boundaries on identity, interaction and exchange	Chapter 8 Key Issue 2
4) Federal and unitary states	Chapter 8 Key Issue 2
5) Spatial relationships between political patterns and patterns of ethnicity, economy, and environment	Chapter 7 Key Issues 2 ,3, and 4; Chapter 8 Key Issue 2
B. Evolution of the contemporary political pattern	
1) Nation-state concept	Chapter 8 Key Issue 1
2) Colonialism and imperialism	Chapter 8 Key Issue 1
3) Democratization	Chapter 8 Key Issues 2 and 3
C. Challenges to political-territorial arrangements	
1) Changing nature of sovereignty	Chapter 7 Key Issue 2
2) Fragmentation, unification, alliance	Chapter 7 Key Issue 2; Chapter 8 Key Issues 2 and 3
3) Supranationalism and devolution	Chapter 7 Key Issue 4; Chapter 8 Key Issue 3
4) Electoral geography, including gerrymandering	Chapter 8 Key Issue 2
5) Terrorism	Chapter 8 Key Issue 4
Unit 5: Agricultural and Rural Land Use	
A. Development and diffusion of agriculture	
1) Neolithic Agricultural Revolution	Chapter 10 Key Issue 1
2) Second Agricultural Revolution	Chapter 12 Key Issues 1 and 2
3) Green Revolution	Chapter 10 Key Issue 4
4) Modern commercial agriculture	Chapter 10 Key Issues 1, 3 and 4
B. Major agricultural production regions	
1) Agricultural systems associated with bioclimatic zones	Chapter 10 Key Issues 1, 2 and 3
2) Variations within major zones and effects of markets	Chapter 10 Key Issues 2 and 3
3) Linkages and flows among regions of food production and consumption	Chapter 10 Key Issue 4
C. Rural land use and settlement patterns	
1) Models of agricultural land us, including von Thunen's model	Chapter 10 Key Issue 4
2) Settlement patterns associated with major agriculture types	Chapter 12 Key Issues 1 and 2
3) Land use/land cover change, irrigation, conservation	Chapter 10 Key Issue 4; Chapter 14 Key Issue 4
D. Modern commercial agriculture	
1) Biotechnology	Chapter 10 Key Issue 4
2) Spatial organization and diffusion of industrial agriculture	Chapter 10 Key Issues 3 and 4
3) Organic farming and local food production	Chapter 10 Key Issue 4
4) Environmental impacts of agriculture	Chapter 10 Key Issue 4; Chapter 14 Key Issue 4
Unit 6: Industrialization and Development	
A. Growth and diffusion of industrialization	
1) Changing role of energy and technology	Chapter 11 Key Issues 1, 3, and 4; Chapter 14 Key Issues 1 and 3
2) Industrial Revolution	Chapter 11 Key Issue 1
3) Evolution of economic cores and peripheries	Chapter 11 Key Issue 1
4) Geographic critiques of models of economic localization, industrial location, economic development and world systems	Chapter 9 Key Issue 4
B. Contemporary patterns and impacts of industrialization and development	
1) Spatial organization of the world economy	Chapter 9 Key Issue 2; Chapter 11 Key Issues 1, 2, 3, and 4
2) Variations in levels of development	Chapter 9 Key Issues 1, 2, and 3
3) Deindustrialization and economic restructuring	Chapter 11 Key Issue 4
4) Globalization and international division of labor	Chapter 11 Key Issues 2 and 4

5) Natural resources and environmental concerns	Chapter 11 Key Issue 3; Chapter 14 Key Issues 1, 2, 3 and 4
6) Sustainable development	Chapter 9 Key Issue 4; Chapter 14 Key Issue 4
7) Local development initiatives: government policies	Chapter 9 Key Issue 4
8) Women in development	Chapter 9 Key Issue 3
Unit 7: Cities and Urban Land Use	
A. Development and character of cities	
1) Origin of cities	Chapter 12 Key Issue 1
2) Rural-urban migration and urban growth	Chapter 3 Key Issue 4; Chapter 12 Key Issue 4
3) Global cities and megacities	Chapter 12 Key Issues 3 and 4
4) Suburbanization and edge cities	Chapter 13 Key Issue 4
B. Models of urban systems	
1) Rank-size rule	Chapter 12 Key Issue 3
2) Central place theory	Chapter 12 Key Issue 3
3) Gravity model	Chapter 12 Key Issue 3
C. Models of internal city structure	
1) Concentric zone model	Chapter 13 Key Issue 2
2) Sector model	Chapter 13 Key Issue 2
3) Multiple-nuclei model	Chapter 13 Key Issue 2
4) Changing employment mix	Chapter 12 Key Issues 1 and 4; Chapter 13 Key Issue 2 and 4
5) Changing demographic and social structures	Chapter 12 Key Issues 2 and 4; Chapter 13 Key Issues 1 and 3
6) Uneven development, ghettoization, and gentrification	Chapter 13 Key Issue 3
D. Built environment and social space	
1) Housing	Chapter 13 Key Issues 3 and 4
2) Transportation and infrastructure	Chapter 13 Key Issues 3 and 4
3) Political organization of urban areas	Chapter 13 Key Issues 3 and 4
4) Urban planning and design	Chapter 13 Key Issues 3 and 4
5) Patterns of race, ethnicity, gender and socioeconomic status	Chapter 7 Key Issue 1; Chapter 13 Key Issues 3 and 4

Upon publication, The Cultural Landscape: An Introduction to Human Geography 10e AP* Edition text was correlated to the College Board's Human Geography Course Description dated May 2010, May 2011. We continually monitor the College Board's AP Course Description for updates to exam topic. For the most current AP Exam Topic correlation for the textbook, visit PearsonSchool.com/AdvancedCorrelations.

About the Authors

John P.A. Hurt graduated from Durham University, UK with a BA (Honours) degree in Geography in 1982. He completed his MEd. in Secondary Education and MA in History at the University of Missouri in St. Louis. John is a Fellow and Chartered Geographer with the United Kingdom's Royal Geographical Society and Institute of British Geographers. He received the National Council for Geographic Education's Distinguished Teaching Award in 1999. John has been teaching geography and history at Heritage High School in Littleton, Colorado since 1993, and Advanced Placement Human Geography since 2000. He is the Social Studies Department Chair at Heritage High School. John is an Endorsed Consultant with The College Board and conducts workshops for AP Human Geography teachers in their Western Region.

Shanna L. Hurt graduated from the University of Texas with a BS degree in Political Science and Secondary Education in 1987. She completed her Masters degree in Geography at East Texas State University. Shanna received the National Council for Geographic Education's Distinguished Teaching Award in 2001. She has been teaching geography, history, and political science in the Littleton Public Schools since 2001, and Advanced Placement Human Geography since 2002. Shanna has been a reader for the AP Human Geography exam since 2006, and has written test items for this exam.

As of August 2010 John and Shanna will be teaching at Seoul International School in Seoul, South Korea.

Chapter 1: Thinking Geographically

Human geographers ask where people and activities are found on Earth and why they are found there. This first chapter introduces the basic concepts that geographers use to answer these questions. These include mapping, place, region, scale, space, and connections.

Key Issue 1 – How Do Geographers Describe Where Things Are?

I. Geography: Its Nature and Perspectives

A. Geography as a field of inquiry

Geography can be divided into two major fields – human geography and physical geography. Physical geography is the study of the physical features and processes on the Earth's surface. The Advanced Placement Human Geography course cannot completely ignore physical geography because the two are integrally connected. For example physical geography influences agricultural decisions, migration patterns, as well as housing choices. Human geography is the scientific study of the **location** of people and activities on the Earth's surface. It is the study of **where** and **why** human activities are located where they are. Geographers look at the world from a **spatial perspective**, and will study how people and objects vary across the Earth's surface. They will also study the relationship or **spatial interaction** between people and objects, as well as the movement or **diffusion** of people and ideas.

The study of human geography involves a consideration of various **scales**. Geographers will observe a tension between **local uniqueness** and **globalizing forces**. This will help to understand many of the world's problems studied in this course, including those related to political conflicts, development and economic geography, and the environment.

I. Geography: Its Nature and Perspectives

B. Evolution of key geographical concepts and models associated with notable geographers

The earliest geographers studied places mainly because of the necessities of trade routes and navigation. The **maps** made by Chinese, Greek, and North African scholars became the foundation of the art and science of map-making or **cartography**. The word *geography* was invented by the ancient Greek scholar Eratosthenes during the third century B.C.; *geo* means "Earth," and *graphy* means "to write." He also accepted the findings of Aristotle and Plato that the earth was round. Two Roman geographers made key contributions to geography. Strabo described the known world in his seventeen-volume work *Geography*. Ptolemy, known as the father of cartography, published numerous maps in his eight-volume *Guide to Geography*.

Geographic inquiry continued during the Middle Ages in the Islamic world, especially through the work of al-Edrisi and Ibn Battuta. European explorers such as the Vikings, Bartholomeu Dias, Christopher Columbus, Vasco Nunez de Balboa, and Ferdinand Magellan traveled and mapped the world beyond their continent.

Geography as a discipline developed from description to explanation and analysis through the work of two German geographers. The philosopher Immanuel Kant had placed geography within an overall framework of scientific knowledge by arguing for logical or physical classification. In the eighteenth century Alexander von Humboldt and Carl Ritter argued for **environmental determinism**, the belief that the environment causes human development.

Later geographers argued that landscapes are the products of complex human-environment relationships. This approach is known as **cultural ecology** or **possibilism**. This approach to the subject recognizes that the physical environment may limit certain human activities, but also that people can adapt to their environment.

The **regional** (or **cultural landscape) studies** approach, which emphasizes the unique characteristics of each place, both human and physical, is a third approach to the study of geography. It was pioneered in the late nineteenth and early twentieth centuries by Paul Vidal de la Blache, Jean Brunhes, Carl Sauer and Robert Platt. While the environmental determinist approach has largely been abandoned by modern geographers, the human-environmental relationships and regional studies approaches remain integral to the scientific study of geography today.

I. Geography: Its Nature and Perspectives

C. Key concepts underlying the geographical perspective: location, space, place, scale, pattern

D. Key geographical skills
1. How to use and think about maps and spatial data
2. How to understand and interpret the implications of associations among phenomena in places
3. How to recognize and interpret at different scales the relationships among patterns and processes

Location and Place

A **place** is the description of a specific point on the Earth's surface; it includes the human and physical features that make it unique. Geographers identify location in one of four ways – place-names, site, situation, and absolute location. All inhabited places on the Earth's surface have been given place-names or **toponyms**. Place-names may tell us about historical origins, such as "Battle" in southern England which is named for the Battle of Hastings. They can also give us an indication of the physical environment such as Aberystwyth in Wales, which means "mouth of the River Ystwyth." Place names may speak to religion, such as Islamabad, Pakistan, or economics such as Gold Point, Nevada. Place-names also change because of political turmoil. The city that was Leningrad in Russia during the Communist era has now been changed back to St. Petersburg.

Site refers to the specific physical characteristics of a place. Site factors such as hilltop, river, and island locations have been important in the historical origins of settlements. The site of Singapore for example is a small, swampy island near to the southern tip of the Malay peninsula. These characteristics can be modified to a certain extent by humans.

Situation or **relative location** describes a place's relationship relative to other places around it. Singapore's relative location near the Strait of Malacca, which is a major passageway between the South China Sea and the Indian Ocean, has been key to its success as a major internationally connected port city.

The exact location or **absolute location** of a place on the earth's surface can be pinpointed on a standard grid or **coordinate system**. This universally accepted system of **latitude** and **longitude** consists of imaginary arcs on a globe. Lines of longitude or **meridians** are drawn between the North and South poles according to a numbering system. 0° is the **prime meridian** which passes through the Royal Observatory at Greenwich, Great Britain. The meridian on the opposite side of the globe is 180° longitude and is called the **International Date Line**. Lines of latitude or **parallels** are circles drawn around the globe parallel to the **equator**. The grid system is especially useful for determining location where there has been no human settlement.

Space and Pattern

Distribution refers to the spatial arrangement of something across the Earth's surface. The three main properties of distribution are density, concentration, and pattern. **Density** is the frequency with which something occurs in an area. The density of anything could be measured, but in the context of human geography it is usually population. The way in which a feature is spread over an area is its **concentration**. Objects that are closer together are **clustered** and those which are further apart are **dispersed**. Again, geographers usually use the concept of concentration in the context of population. **Pattern** is the geometric arrangement of objects which could be regular or irregular. For example geographers could describe the regular pattern of streets in American and Canadian cities as a grid pattern.

Scale

Map **scale** refers to the ratio between the distance on a map and the actual distance on the Earth's surface. Scale is usually presented by cartographers as a fraction (1/24,000), a ratio (1:24,000), or a written statement ("1 inch equals 1 mile"). In a **small-scale** map, the ratio between maps units and ground units is small (such as 1:100,000) and since one map unit equals so many of the same units on the ground, these maps tend to cover large regions (such as a map of the United States). In a **large-scale** map, the ratio between map units and ground units is large (such as 1:5,000) and thus cover much smaller regions (such as a map of a city).

Projection

A map can be used as a **reference tool**, to learn where something is found and to navigate from one place to another. Maps can also be used as a **communication tool**, to depict the location of human activities and physical features, as well as to explain their distribution. Globes are relatively impractical for these uses; thus most maps are flat. The scientific method of transferring the Earth to a flat map is called a **projection**, and inevitably involves some distortion. There are three general classes of map projections: **conic**, **cylindrical**, and **planar** (or **azimuthal**) as well as a fourth, a false cylindrical class with an **oval** shape. The shape of an area, the distance between two points, the relative size of different areas, and the direction from one place to another are the types of distortion that can result.

Most of the world maps in Rubenstein's text are **equal area projections** because the relative size of an area is kept the same although shapes are distorted. **Conformal maps** distort area but not shape. The uninterrupted **Robinson projection** allocates space to oceans but shows land areas much smaller than on interrupted maps of the same size. The **Mercator projection** minimizes the distortion of shape and direction but grossly distorts area toward the poles, making high latitude places look much larger than they actually are.

I. Geography: Its Nature and Perspectives

E. New geographic technologies, such as GIS, remote sensing, and GPS

F. Sources of geographical ideas and data: the field, census data, and satellite imagery

Important technologies related to geography that have been developed since the 1970's include **remote sensing**, the **Global Positioning System (GPS)**, and **Geographical Information Systems (GIS)**. Remote sensing is the process of acquiring data about the Earth's surface from satellites. This could include the mapping of vegetation, winter ice, or changes in weather patterns or deforestation. A GPS device enables one to determine absolute location through an integrated network of satellites. It also allows geographers to determine distances between two points and is thus a valuable navigational tool. GIS enables geographers to map, analyze, and process different pieces of information about a location. These **thematic layers** could include various physical features, transportation infrastructure, population and settlement patterns, and could be analyzed individually or together. Indeed GIS is especially useful when relationships can be seen between the different layers. This is a more sophisticated and technological version of a **thematic map** such as a **choropleth map** (a color coded map used to show the distribution of a geographic phenomena over space).

Key Issue 2 – Why Is Each Point on Earth Unique?

I. Geography: Its Nature and Perspectives

C. Key concepts underlying the geographical perspective: regionalization

D. Key geographic skills
4. How to define regions and evaluate the regionalization process

A **region** is generally defined as an area larger than a single city that contains unifying cultural and/or physical characteristics. The concept is controversial because geographers will debate what exactly makes a region. However it is important as a basic unit of geographic research and a necessary simplification of the world for geographic examination. Geographers have identified three types of regions: formal, functional, and vernacular.

A **formal region** is also called a **uniform region** or a **homogeneous region** because it has specific characteristics that are fairly uniform throughout that region. For example Colorado is a political region and the Rocky Mountains constitute a physical region. North Africa and the Middle East constitute a formal region characterized by a desert climate as well as an Arab/Islamic culture.

A **functional region** is also called a **nodal region** because it is defined by a social or economic function that occurs between a node or focal point and the surrounding areas. For example the circulation area of the Denver Post is a functional region and Denver is the node.

A **vernacular region** or **perceptual region** is one that exists in people's minds such as the American "South." When individuals are asked to draw a boundary around this region, their boundary will probably be based on stereotypes they associate with the South such as climate, accent, cuisine, and religious practices such as Southern Baptist. It would be difficult to determine the precise boundary of the South. One's attachment to a region perceived as home is sometimes called a **sense of place**. Sometimes people can identify their perceptual region by envisioning or drawing a **mental map**. A mental map is an internal representation of a place on the Earth's surface.

Key Issue 3 – Why are different places similar?

I. Geography: Its Nature and Perspectives

C. Key concepts underlying the geographical perspective: globalization

Spatial interaction and interdependence have become increasingly important concepts in geography because of **globalization**, which is the idea that the world is becoming interdependent on a global scale to the extent that smaller scales are becoming less important. It produces a more uniform world.

I. Geography: Its Nature and Perspectives

D. Key geographical skills
5. How to characterize and analyze changing interconnections among places

Economic globalization has led to an increase in **transnational corporations** that invest and operate in many countries. Modern communication and transportation systems have made it much easier to move economic assets around the world. Economically some places are more connected than others. **Complementarity** is the degree to which one place can supply something that another place needs. The concept of **intervening opportunities** also helps to explain connectivity. It is the idea that if one place has a demand for something and there are two potential suppliers, the closer supplier will represent an intervening opportunity because transportation costs will be less. Thus **accessibility** is an important factor in costs and interaction between places. **Transferability** refers to the costs involved in moving goods from one place to another.

There will generally be more interaction between things that are closer than those that are further away. This is **Tobler's First Law of Geography** or the **friction of distance**. Contact will diminish with increasing distance until it ultimately disappears. This is called **distance decay**.

As a result of globalization, there are now greater communications between distant places. **Time-space compression** describes the reduction in time that it takes to diffuse something to a distant place.

Spatial diffusion describes the way that phenomena, such as technological ideas, cultural innovations, disease, or economic goods, travel over space. The place from which an innovation originates and diffuses is called a **hearth**. **Relocation diffusion** or **migration diffusion** refers to the physical movement of people from one place to another. It will be discussed later in the context of migration.

Expansion diffusion is the spread of something in a snowballing process. There are three types of expansion diffusion. **Hierarchical diffusion** is the spread of an idea from one node of power and authority to another. For example trends in music, fashion, and art are more likely to diffuse hierarchically from one key city to another (such as from New York to Los Angeles). **Contagious diffusion** is the rapid and widespread diffusion of something throughout a population because of proximity, such as a contagious disease like influenza. **Stimulus diffusion** is the spread of a principle rather than a specific characteristic.

KEY TERMS

Absolute location	Clustered
Accessibility	Complementarity
Cartography	Concentration
Choropleth map	Conformal maps

Contagious diffusion
Coordinate system
Cultural ecology
Density
Diffusion
Dispersed
Distance decay
Distribution
Environmental determinism
Equal area projection
Equator
Expansion diffusion
Formal region
Friction of distance
Functional region
Geographical Information Systems
(GIS)
Globalization
Globalizing forces
Global Positioning System (GPS)
Hearth
Hierarchical diffusion
Homogeneous region
International Date Line
Intervening opportunities
Large-scale
Latitude
Local uniqueness
Location
Longitude
Map
Map as a communication tool
Map as a reference tool
Map projection
Mental Map
Mercator projection

Meridians
Migration diffusion
Nodal region
Parallels
Pattern
Perceptual region
Possibilism
Place
Prime meridian
Region
Regional (or cultural landscape)
studies
Relative location
Relocation diffusion
Remote sensing
Robinson projection
Scale
Sense of place
Site
Situation
Small-scale
Space
Spatial diffusion
Spatial interaction
Spatial perspective
Stimulus diffusion
Thematic layers
Thematic map
Time-space compression
Tobler's First Law of Geography
Toponyms
Transferability
Transnational corporations
Uniform region
Vernacular region

Key Issues Revisited

1. How do geographers describe where things are?
-geographers use maps to display the location of objects and to get information about places
-early geographers drew maps of the Earth based on exploration and observation
-GIS and other contemporary technological tools help geographers to understand what they see on the Earth's surface

2. Why is each point on Earth unique?

-every place in the world has a unique location on the Earth's surface

-geographers identify regions as areas distinguished by a distinctive combination of cultural, economic, and environmental features which helps us to understand why every region and place is unique

3. Why are different places similar?

-geographers work at all scales, from local to global, and the global scale is becoming increasingly important because few places in today's world are completely isolated

-places display similarities because they are connected to each other

-geographers study the interactions of people and human activities across space, and they identify the different processes by which people and ideas diffuse from one place to another over time

Chapter 2: Population

This chapter describes **population distribution**, the spatial distribution of people on the Earth's surface, and where population is growing. The chapter then explains why population is growing at different rates in different places. It discusses the extent to which certain regions of the world may be facing an overpopulation problem.

Key Issue 1: Where Is The World's Population Distributed?

II. Population

A. Geographical analysis of population
1. Density, distribution, and scale

The study of population geography or **demography** is very important because there are more than six billion people alive today, the growth of the world's population has been most rapid in the last century, and the fastest growth today is in the developing world. Population related issues are key to other chapters especially development, agriculture, and urbanization.

Two-thirds of the world's population is clustered in four regions – East Asia, South Asia, Southeast Asia, and Western Europe. The clustering of the world's population can be shown on a **cartogram**, which depicts the size of countries according to population rather than land area. Approximately two-thirds of the world's population lives within 500 kilometers of an ocean. China and India each have over a billion people and together hold over one-third of the world's population. The largest percentages of people in Asia live in rural areas whereas three-quarters of all Europeans live in towns and cities.

The above overview of world population is at a global level and thus necessarily generalized. The analysis of population patterns at different scales, including continental, national, state or provincial, and local will reveal different trends and patterns.

The harsh physical environments of the Earth's surface, including deserts, tropical rainforests, mountain, and polar regions, are understandably sparsely populated. The portion of the Earth's surface occupied by permanent human settlement is called the **ecumene**.

Arithmetic density (also called **population density**) is a misleading measure of the distribution of people because it is the total number of people divided by the total land area. For example to say that the arithmetic population density of Egypt is 75 people per square kilometer (195 people per square mile) hides the fact that the vast majority of that country's population live in the delta and valley of the Nile River, and much of the country is virtually uninhabited.

Physiological density is a more useful measure of population because it is the number of people supported by a unit area of arable land. The physiological population density of Egypt is 2,580 people per square kilometer (6,682 people per square mile), which is a very good measure of the pressure on agricultural land in that country.

Agricultural density is the ratio of the number of farmers to the amount of agricultural land. Countries like Canada and the United States have much lower agricultural densities than less developed countries like India and Bangladesh. In more developed countries technology related to agriculture allows a few farmers to work huge area of land and feed many people. Thus agricultural density and physiological density are good measures of the relationship between population and resources together with the level of development in a country.

Key Issue 2 – Where has the world's population increased?

II. Population

B. Population growth and decline over time and space
1. Historical trends and projections for the future

The crude birth rate, crude death rate, and rate of natural increase are used to measure population change in a country. The **crude birth rate (CBR)** or **natality rate** and **crude death rate (CDR)** are statistical terms that refer to the total number of live births and deaths respectively, per thousand people in a country. Where the CBR is higher than the CDR, **natural increase (NIR)** occurs. This does not account for migration. If the CDR is about the same as the CBR a country has **zero population growth (ZPG)**. If the CDR is higher than the CBR, there is a **negative NIR**. The **demographic equation** is the global difference between births and deaths.

During the first decade of the twenty-first century the world rate of natural increase was 1.2, which meant that the world's population was growing each year by 1.2%. It would take the world fifty-four years to double its population given this rate of growth; this is called **doubling time**. During the 1960's and 1970's the world's doubling time was about thirty-five years.

It is important to understand there are major regional differences in rates of population growth. The NIR exceeds 3% in many countries in sub-Saharan Africa. Indeed most of the world's population growth is now in developing countries. At the other extreme some Western European countries are now experiencing negative population growth. China, the most populous country in the world, has done much in terms of government mandates to lower its population growth rates. India will soon surpass China as the most populous country in the world.

II. Population

B. Population growth and decline over time and space
3. Patterns of fertility, mortality, and health

The highest crude birth rates are in Africa and the lowest are in Europe and North America. The **total fertility rate (TFR)** is used by demographers to measure the number of births in a country. The TFR is the average number of children a woman will have during her childbearing years (ages 15 through 49). TFRs exceed six in some countries in sub-Saharan Africa.

The **infant mortality rate (IMR)** is the annual number of deaths of infants under one year of age, compared with total live births, and is usually expressed as number of deaths per 1,000 births. IMR is a measure of a country's level of health care, and the highest rates are in less developed countries. The other useful measure of mortality is **life**

expectancy. This is the number of years a newborn infant can expect to live at current mortality levels. Life expectancy rates are sometimes twice as high in developed countries than in developing countries.

Key Issue 3 – Why is population increasing at different rates in different countries?

II. Population

B. Population growth and decline over time and space
2. Theories of population growth, including the demographic transition model
4. Regional variations of demographic transitions

The **demographic transition model** explains changes in the natural increase rate as a function of economic development. It is a process with four stages, and every country is in one of them.

Stage 1 of the demographic transition is one of high birth rates and death rates and consequently very low growth. Most of human history was spent in stage 1 but no countries remain in that stage today.

Stage 2 is one of high growth or **demographic momentum** because death rates decline and birth rates remain high. Demographic momentum will be sustained because of a relatively young population. The demographic transition assumes that countries enter stage 2 because they go through the **industrial revolution**. Technologies associated with industry helped countries to produce more food and improve sanitation and health. Western European countries and North America entered stage 2 after 1750. Countries in Latin America, Asia, and Africa have experienced stage 2 much more recently, and without experiencing an industrial revolution. The rapid increase in population associated with stage 2 is often referred to as a **population explosion**. Developing countries have moved into stage 2 because of a **medical revolution**, the diffusion of medical technologies to LDCs. The sudden decline in death rates that comes from technological innovations has now occurred everywhere.

Countries will move from stage 2 to stage 3 when their crude birth rates drop sharply as a result of changes in social and economic patterns that will encourage people to have fewer children. The demographic transition assumes that people in stage 3 are more likely to live in nuclear families in an urban and industrial world. Chile is in stage 3 of the demographic transition. The drop in birth rates that comes with changes in social customs has yet to be achieved in many countries.

Countries will reach stage 4 of the demographic transition because their birth rates will continue to decline until the natural increase rate drops to zero. This is true of countries in Europe together with Canada, Australia, and Japan. The demographic transition assumes that this occurs because of more changes in social customs such as women entering the labor force in larger numbers.

It could be argued that some countries, primarily Western and Northern European, that are now experiencing population decline, have entered a stage 5 for which the demographic transition does not account.

II. Population

A. Geographical analysis of population
3. Patterns of composition: age, sex, race, and ethnicity

The **age-sex distribution (ratio)** of a country's population can be shown on a **population pyramid**. It will show the distribution of a country's population between males and females of various ages. A population pyramid will normally show the percentage of the total population in five-year age groups, with the youngest group at the base of the pyramid and the oldest group at the top. Males are usually shown on the left and females on the right. Each age-sex group is called a population **cohort**. Population pyramids can tell us much about the population history of a country. A pyramid with a wide base shows a rapidly growing country with a large proportion of young people, and is typical of a less developed county. A pyramid that is more rectangular depicts a country with a relatively even number of young, middle-aged, and older people, and is typical of a more developed country. Population pyramids are also useful tools to analyze and predict future population growth. Such a usage is referred to as **population projection**.

The **dependency ratio** is the percentage of people in a population who are either too old (over 65) or young (0-14) to work and thus, must be supported by others.

Key Issue 4 – Why might the world face an overpopulation problem?

II. Population

A. Geographical analysis of population
2. Implications of various densities and distributions

B. Population growth and decline over time and space
1. Historical trends and projections for the future
2. Theories of population growth

One of the most famous models to explain changes in population over time was developed by Thomas Malthus. Malthus was an English economist and demographer who published *Essay on the Principle of Population* in 1798. He argued that the world's population was growing geometrically or **exponentially**, but food supplies were only growing arithmetically. According to Malthus this would lead to "negative checks" consisting of starvation and disease because of a lack of food. The only way to avoid this would be for populations to lower crude birth rates.

Malthus' theory is still potentially relevant today because of rapid population growth in some LDCs. His adherents today are called **neo-Malthusians** and are led by Paul Ehrlich who has made a similar argument to Malthus in *The Population Bomb*. Neo-Malthusians such as Robert Kaplan and Thomas Fraser Homer-Dixon have broadened Malthus' theory to include fuel, agricultural land and other resources as well as food.

Malthus has his critics too. The Marxist theorist Friedrich Engels believes that the world has enough resources to eliminate hunger and poverty if they are more equally shared. Contemporary critics include Julian Simon and Esther Boserup who argue that larger populations can actually stimulate economic growth. Malthus was terribly pessimistic and did not foresee the development of new agricultural technologies, or the human ability to reduce population growth rates.

II. Population

B. Population growth and decline over time and space
5. Effects of population policies

Most demographers would agree that some parts of the world are **overpopulated,** where a country can no longer sustainably support its population because it has reached its carrying capacity. In human geography **carrying capacity** refers to the number of people a given area can support.

The CBR has declined rapidly since 1990 except in some countries in sub-Saharan Africa. This has occurred partly as a result of economic development which has resulted in more money for education and health care. Birth rates have also been lowered because of diffusion of modern contraceptives. Some countries, such as Bangladesh, have reduced their birth rates like this without economic development. There is opposition to birth-control programs from some countries for religious and political reasons.

II. Population

B. Population growth and decline over time and space
2. Theories of population growth
3. Patterns of fertility, mortality, and health

Medical researchers have identified an **epidemiologic transition** that focuses on the causes of death in each stage of the demographic transition. **Epidemiology** is the branch of medicine that is concerned with disease. In stage 1 of the epidemiologic transition, infectious and parasitic diseases were the main causes of death. These include the Black Plague and cholera **pandemics**. A pandemic occurs over a very wide geographic area unlike an **epidemic** which is more localized. These causes of death were most common for people in countries in stage 1 and the early part of stage 2 of the demographic transition.

Stage 3 of the epidemiologic transition is associated with degenerative and human-created diseases such as heart diseases and cancer. As LDCs have moved from stage 2 to stage 3 of the demographic transition, the incidence of infectious diseases has declined. Human-created diseases are more typical of countries in stage 4 of the demographic transition.

Some medical researchers have argued that the world is now moving into stage 5 of the epidemiologic transition, characterized by a reemergence of infectious and parasitic diseases. This could be for a number of reasons including the evolution of infectious disease microbes, poverty, and improved travel. Avian flu is one of the "new" infectious diseases that has emerged in recent decades, and it has the potential to become pandemic. However, AIDS is the most lethal epidemic of recent years, especially in sub-Saharan Africa where there were more than 25 million people infected with HIV in 2005.

KEY TERMS

Age-sex distribution (ratio)

Agricultural density

Arithmetic density

Carrying capacity

Cartogram

Cohort

Crude birth rate (CBR)

Crude death rate (CDR)

Demographic equation

Demographic momentum

Demographic transition model

Demography

Dependency ratio

Doubling time

Ecumene

Epidemic

Epidemiologic transition

Epidemiology

Exponentially

Industrial Revolution

Infant mortality rate (IMR)

Life expectancy

Medical revolution

Natality rate

Natural increase rate (NIR)

Neo-Malthusian

Overpopulated

Pandemic

Physiological density

Population density

Population distribution

Population explosion

Population projection

Population pyramid

Thomas Malthus

Total fertility rate (TFR)

Zero population growth (ZPG)

Key Issues Revisited

1. Where is the world's population distributed?
-the world's population is concentrated in a few places
-people tend to avoid places that they consider to be too wet, too dry, too cold, or too mountainous

2. Where has the world's population increased?
-most of the world's natural increase is in the LDCs of Africa, Asia, and Latin America
-most European and North American countries now have low population growth rates, and some are experiencing population decline
-the difference in rates of natural increase between MDCs and LDCs is mainly due to differences in CBRs rather than CDRs

3. Why is population increasing at different rates in different countries?
-the demographic transition shows the change in a country's population. According to this model a country will move from a situation of high birth and death rates, with little population growth, to one of low birth and death rates, with low population growth
-through the demographic transition, the total population increases tremendously, because the death rate declines some years before the birth rate does
-the MDCs of Europe and North America have reached stage four of the demographic transition

-African, Asian, and Latin American countries are at stage two or three of the demographic transition where population growth is rapid, death rates have declined sharply, but birth rates remain relatively high

4. Why might the world face an overpopulation problem?
-as a result of a dramatic decline in the death rate, global population grew at an unprecedented rate during the second half of the twentieth century
-birth rates began to decline sharply during the 1990's, slowing world population growth and reducing fears of overpopulation in most regions
-demographers agree that the current rate of natural increase must be further reduced, but they disagree on the methods to achieve this goal

Chapter 3: Migration

The chapter focuses on migration which is a specific type of relocation diffusion. It examines why people move permanently or migrate, both internally and internationally. Migration patterns are analyzed as well as the obstacles faced by migrants.

Key Issue 1 – Why do people migrate?

II. Population

A. Geographical analysis of population
4. Population and natural hazards: past, present, and future

C. Population movement
1. Migration selectivity
3. Theories of migration
4. International migration and refugees
5. Socioeconomic consequences of migration

E.G. Ravenstein, a nineteenth century geographer, identified eleven laws of migration which can be roughly organized into three main elements: the reasons migrants move, the distance they move, and the major characteristics of migration. Migration is a specific type of relocation diffusion and is a form of **mobility,** a more general term dealing with all types of movement. **Migration** is the movement of a person from one place to another. It can include movement at many different scales, such as short-term, repetitive, or cyclical movements called **circulation**, or **intercontinental migration**, which is from one continent to another. **Emigration** is movement *from* a location whereas **immigration** is movement *to* a location. The difference between the number of immigrants and the number of emigrants is the **net migration**.

People generally migrate because of push and pull factors. **Push factors** include anything that would want to cause someone to leave their present location, such as the violation of a person's **activity space. Pull factors** induce people to move to a new location. Four major kinds of push and pull factors can be identified. These are economic, political, cultural, and environmental.

Economic factors that can lead to migration include job opportunities, cycles of economic growth and recession, and cost of living. The United States and Canada have been important destinations for economic migrants lured by economic pull factors. An example of this is **place utility**, where a place may offer economic incentives in an effort to attract people to their town or city.

Armed conflict and the policies of oppressive regimes have been important political push factors in forcing out those who become refugees. **Refugees**, according to the United Nations are people who, "owing to well-founded fear of being persecuted for reasons of race, religion, nationality, membership in a particular social group, or political

30

opinion, is outside the country of his nationality, and is unable to or, owing to such fear, is unwilling to avail himself of the protection of that country." Of the more than thirty-three million refugees in the world, more than two-thirds of them are from Asia and Africa. There are also political pull factors such as the promise of political freedom. It has been this factor that has lured so many people from the Communist countries of Eastern Europe to Western Europe in the second half of the twentieth century.

Cultural factors can encourage people to move to places where they will be more at home culturally. A good example of a cultural pull factor is the relocation of Jews to the newly formed state of Israel after the Second World War. Israel is the ancestral hearth of Jewish culture and it serves as a place where Jewish people can reestablish social ties and create a sense of political unity.

Environmental pull and push factors are largely related to physical geography. People will be pulled towards physically attractive regions such as the Rocky Mountains and the Mediterranean coast of southern Europe. People might also be pushed from places by floods and droughts. The flooding in New Orleans and other Gulf coast communities in 2005 following Hurricane Katrina caused around 1,400 deaths and forced several hundred thousand people from their homes. Indeed many people are forced to move by water-related disasters because they live in vulnerable areas, such as a **floodplain**.

Migrants do not always go to their intended destination because of an **intervening obstacle**, which is an environmental or cultural feature that hinders migration. Sometimes a migrant will stop and stay at a place en route to their intended destination because of an **intervening opportunity**, which is an environmental or cultural feature that favors migration.

II. Population

2. Major voluntary and involuntary migrations at different scales

According to Ravenstein, most migrants move only a short distance and within a country. **Internal migration** is permanent movement within a country. This is the most common type of movement and is consistent with the principles of distance decay. **Interregional migration** is one type of internal migration, and is movement from one region of a country to another. Historically this has usually been from rural to urban, but developed countries are now experiencing more urban to rural migration. The other type of internal migration is **intraregional migration**, movement within a region. In the developed world this has largely been urban to suburban but these patterns are now beginning to change.

One of Ravenstein's laws states that long-distance migrants to other countries usually relocate to major economic and urban centers. The permanent migration from one country to another is **international migration**, and it can be voluntary or forced. **Voluntary migration** is when someone chooses to leave a place as a result of push or pull factors. **Forced migration** is when someone is moved from their home without any choice.

A century ago Ravenstein stated that most long-distance migrants were male adults rather than families with children. Today there are much larger numbers of females migrating internationally together with their children, especially from Mexico to the United States. This is a reflection of the changing role of women. Much of the migration from Mexico to the United States is illegal and seasonal.

II. Population

B. Population growth and decline over time and space
2. Theories of population

C. Population Movement
3. Theories of migration

The demographer Wilbur Zelinsky has identified a **migration transition** which outlines changes in the migration pattern in a society during different stages of the demographic transition. According to the migration transition, international migration usually occurs when countries are in stage two of the demographic transition. For example, international migrants moved from Western Europe to the United States as a result of the technological changes related to the Industrial Revolution. Internal migration becomes more important when countries are in stages three and four of the demographic transition. According to migration transition theory, people generally move from cities to suburbs during these stages. Zelinsky theorizes that countries in stages three and four of the demographic transition are the destinations of international migrants leaving stage two counties because of economic push and pull factors.

Key Issue 2 – Where are migrants distributed?

II. Population

C. Population movement
2. Major voluntary and involuntary migrations at different scales
5. Socioeconomic consequences of migration

At a global scale people generally migrate from the developing to the developed world. The three largest flows are from Asia to Europe and North America, and from Latin America.

More than most other countries, the United States is a land of immigrants. About 75 million people migrated to the United States between 1820 and 2010. There have been three major eras of immigration to the United States. The first era was the original settlement of colonies in the 1600's. The second was from the mid nineteenth century to the early twentieth century, and the third was from the 1970's until the present. All three eras have involved people coming to the United States from countries that were at stage two of the demographic transition.

Immigration to the American colonies consisted of mostly forced migration from Africa and a mixture of forced and voluntary migration from Europe. There were three peaks of the second era of immigration. The first peak of immigration was during the 1840's and 1850's and consisted of people largely from Western Europe. The second peak was during the late 1800's and again most migrants were from Western Europe, especially Germany and Ireland, although there were increasing numbers of people from Scandinavia. The third peak was from the late 1800's until the early 1900's and consisted of people largely from Southern and Eastern Europe who came to work in the factories of the Industrial Revolution.

Recent immigration to the United States has been from less developed regions, especially Asia and Latin America. The three leading sources of U.S. immigrants from Asia are China, India, and the Philippines. In the 1980's Mexico became the leading source of immigrants to the U.S. Although the pattern of immigration to the U.S. has changed, the reason for immigration remains essentially the same. People are pushed from their homeland by economic and political conditions, and are attracted to the economic and social potential of life in the U.S.

Today's immigrants to the U.S. are clustered in California, New York, Florida, and Texas. New immigrants often move to places where family members and friends from their home country have already migrated. This is called **chain migration**.

There have been increasing numbers of illegal, **unauthorized**, or **undocumented immigrants** to the United States. In 2005 the Urban Institute estimated that there may have been as many as 9.3 million undocumented immigrants, including 5.3 million from Mexico. It is a controversial topic because although undocumented immigrants take jobs that few others want, most Americans would also like more effective border patrols. Thus some favor **amnesty** for illegal immigrants whereas others believe that they should be deported.

Key Issue 3 – Why do migrants face obstacles?

II. Population

B. Population growth and decline over time and space
5. Effects of population policies

C. Population movement
5. Socioeconomic consequences of migration

The United States uses a quota system to limit the number of foreign citizens who can migrate permanently to the country. **Quotas** are maximum limits on the number of people who can immigrate to the U.S. from one country during a one-year period. Initial quota laws were designed to allow more Europeans to come to the U.S., rather than Asians. Quotas for individual countries were eliminated in 1968 and replaced with hemisphere quotas. In 1978 the hemisphere quotas were replaced by a global quota. The majority of legal immigration today is chain migration. Some preference is also given to skilled workers, which leads to **brain drain**, the emigration of talented people. According to the World Bank in 2005 85% of Haitians with a college degree lived abroad.

Europe allows temporary **guest workers** to legally work for at least minimum wages in their countries. They serve the same purpose as the vast majority of illegal immigrants in the U.S. Luxembourg and Switzerland have especially high percentages of foreign born workers in their labor force. Between 1999 and 2008, the foreign-born population in Spain rose from around ¾ million to 5¼ million.

In the 19th century **time-contract** workers migrated to work in mines and on plantations for a set period of time, although many of them stayed. More than 33 million ethnic Chinese currently live in other countries. Thus it is sometimes difficult to distinguish between economic migrants and refugees.

The U.S. has generally regarded emigrants from Cuba as political refugees since Castro's 1959 revolution. Economic and political refugees from Haiti have not been quite as welcome in the U.S. Vietnamese boat people were regarded as political refugees after the Vietnam War when thousands fled the war ravaged country. Vietnam remains an important source of immigrants to the United States today, but largely because of the pull of economic opportunity rather than the push of political persecution.

Immigrants often face opposition from some citizens of host countries because they are often culturally, ethnically and religiously different. For example there have been open ethnic and racial conflicts between citizens and migrants in Western Europe and Australia in the first decade of the 21st century.

Key Issue 4 – Why do people migrate within a country?

II. Population

C. Population movement
1. Migration selectivity
2. Major voluntary and involuntary migrations
3. Theories of migration
5. Socioeconomic consequences of migration

Historically the most significant migration trend has been **interregional migration** westward in United States to obtain cheap land and potential wealth. The population center of the U.S. has moved westward and, more recently southward. In the 1960's and 1970's large numbers of white, middle-class Americans moved from the older northeastern and midwestern to the south and the west coast. At this time northern industrial states were known as the **Rust Belt** because their economy was declining as factories closed and people moved. At the same time the south, which had been known as the **Cotton Belt** because of its agricultural poverty, became known as the **Sun Belt**, a land of opportunity. The migration of African-Americans followed a different pattern, from the rural south to large cities in the north. Interregional migration in the U.S. has not been as significant in the first decade of the twenty-first century, largely because of a narrowing of regional differences in employment opportunities.

Interregional migration has also been important in other countries. Soviet policy encouraged people to move to Russia's Far North to develop industry. It didn't work very well and ended with the collapse of the Soviet Union. Brazil has encouraged people to move into the interior, especially since the building of Brasilia in 1960. Since 1969 the Indonesian government has paid for the migration of more than five million people from the island of Java to less populated islands.

Intraregional migration has also been important in many countries. In the United States as well as most MDCs, the most important trend since the middle of the 20th century has been the move to suburbs from central cities. A new trend in North America and Western Europe has been **counterurbanization**, from urban to rural areas for lifestyle preferences especially now that modern technology allows people to work more easily from their homes.

Migration from rural to urban areas has been very important in LDCs. Worldwide more than 20 million people are estimated to migrate each year from rural to urban areas. People seek economic opportunities with this type of migration and, especially in LDCs, are pushed because of failed agricultural systems.

KEY TERMS

Activity space

Amnesty

Brain drain

Chain migration

Circulation

Cotton Belt

Counterurbanization

Emigration

Floodplain

Forced migration

Guest workers

Immigration

Intercontinental migration

Internal migration

International migration

Interregional migration

Intervening obstacle

Intervening opportunity

Intraregional migration

Migration

Migration transition

Mobility

Net migration

Place utility

Pull factors

Push factors

Quotas

Refugees

Rust Belt

Sun Belt

Time-contract workers

Unauthorized immigrants

Undocumented immigration

Voluntary migration

Key Issues Revisited

1. Why do people migrate?
-push factors include emigration from a location for political, economic, and environmental reasons
-pull factors include immigration for political, economic, and environmental factors
-we can distinguish between international and internal migration

2. Where are migrants distributed?
-at a global scale, the largest flows of migrants are from Asia to Europe and from Asia and Latin America to the United States
-the United States receives by far the largest number of migrants

3. Why do migrants face obstacles?
-migrants have difficulty getting permission to enter other countries, and often face hostility from local citizens once they arrive
-immigration laws restrict the number who can legally enter the United States
-guest workers migrate temporarily to perform menial jobs in Europe and the Middle East

4. Why do people migrate within a country?
-there is both interregional and intraregional migration within a country
-historically, interregional migration was important in settling the frontier of large countries such as the United States, Russia, and Brazil
-the most important intraregional trends are from rural to urban areas within LDCs, and from cities to suburbs within MDCs

38

Chapter 4: Folk and Popular Culture

Rubenstein defines culture as the body of customary beliefs, social forms, and material traits that together constitute a group of people's distinct tradition. Culture can be distinguished from habit and custom. A **habit** is a repetitive act that an individual performs and a **custom** is a repetitive act of a group. Culture combines three things – values, material artifacts, and political institutions. This chapter deals with the material artifacts of culture or **material culture**, which includes the **built environment** or visible objects that a group possesses and leaves behind for the future. It will focus on the two basic categories, folk and popular culture, their origins, diffusion, and spatial distribution. Popular culture has a more widespread distribution than folk culture, and its globalization causes problems that are addressed here.

Key Issue 1 – Where do folk and popular cultures originate and diffuse?

III. Cultural Patterns and Processes

A. Concepts of culture
1. Traits

B. Cultural differences
5. Popular and folk culture

  Folk culture refers to the cultural practices of small, homogeneous groups living in traditional societies. Folk cultures are usually isolated and rural, with subsistence economies. Distinctive architecture and other material artifacts such as tools, musical instruments, and clothing contribute to the uniqueness of folk cultures. Nonmaterial aspects of folk culture include songs (**folk songs**), stories (**folklore**), and belief systems. Folk cultures originate in multiple **hearths** because of their isolation.
  Popular culture on the other hand, refers to the cultural practices of large, heterogeneous societies that share many habits and characteristics. The elements of popular culture look similar in different places, and result in a relatively uniform landscape. Artifacts include music, food, entertainment, fashion, recreation, and various forms of art.

III. Cultural Patterns and Processes

A. Concepts of Culture
2. Diffusion

  Folk culture diffuses slowly, on a small scale, usually through **relocation diffusion**. The Amish culture in the United States is a good example of the diffusion of a folk culture. Popular culture is easily diffused around the world, largely through **hierarchical diffusion**. The globalization of soccer is an example of the transformation and diffusion of an English folk culture to a popular culture.
Key Issue 2 – Why is folk culture clustered?

III. Cultural Patterns and Processes

B. Cultural differences
5. Folk culture

C. Cultural landscapes and cultural identity
1. Values and preferences
2. Symbolic landscapes and sense of place

Folk cultures are practiced by many different groups living in relative isolation. They are especially susceptible to the various ways in which the physical environment can limit their activities and diffusion, because of their low level of technology. Thus their cultural identity and landscapes will be very diverse. For example there are many different types of Himalayan art in a relatively small geographic area because of the harsh physical environment and limited interaction. Housing provides another good example of the diversity of folk culture that results from the interaction of cultural and physical geography. The resultant landscapes exemplify distinctive and unique senses of place.

III. Cultural Patterns and Processes

C. Cultural landscapes and cultural identity
3. Environmental impact of cultural attitudes and practices

Cultural traits such as food, clothing, and housing are influenced by physical geography. Folk cultural traits, such as housing (**folk housing** or **indigenous architecture**) are especially responsive to the environment because of their low level of technology and utilization of available resources. The sum of the effects of the local environment on a specific food item is called **terroir**. It is commonly used to describe the way in which soil, climate, and other physical features influence the character of distinctive wines. Restrictions on certain behaviors, like the consumption of particular foods, can also be imposed by social customs. This is called a **taboo**.

Key Issue 3 – Why is popular culture widely distributed?

III. Cultural Patterns and Processes

A. Concepts of culture
2. Diffusion

B. Cultural differences
5. Popular culture

Popular culture diffuses rapidly where high levels of technology allow people to acquire material possessions. The increasingly global world allows for the rapid diffusion and acceptance of the material and nonmaterial elements of popular culture. For example, as a result of the diffusion of popular culture, there are less regional differences in housing, clothing and food in more developed countries. Television has played a major role in the diffusion of popular culture, especially since World War Two. International rates of TV ownership have climbed rapidly in LDCs in the early twenty-first century, but there are still international differences in TV ownership.

In the last decade other electronic media have become important transmitters of popular culture. Internet service has diffused at a rapid pace, from 40 million Internet users worldwide in 1995 to 1.6 billion in 2008. Since its founding in 2004 Facebook has also diffused rapidly, and had 200 million active users by 2009.

Key Issue 4 – Why does globalization of popular culture cause problems?

III. Cultural Patterns and Processes

B. Cultural differences
4. Gender
5. Popular and folk culture

The traditional role of women in developing counties is changing as a result of the diffusion of popular culture. It is leading to the advancement of women through education, economic and social opportunities. However it may also lead to negative impacts such as sex crimes against women.

III. Cultural Patterns and Processes

C. Cultural landscapes and cultural identity
1. Values and preferences

The diffusion of popular culture threatens the survival of folk culture. It is one example of **cultural imperialism**, causing people to lose their traditional ways of life in favor of the material elements of popular culture from more developed countries. For example the western dominance of the television industry, especially the news media, threatens the independence of less developed countries. Three MDCs – the United States, the United Kingdom, and Japan – dominate the television industry in LDCs. The diffusion of information to newspapers around the world is dominated by the Associated Press (AP) and Reuters, which are owned by U.S. and British companies respectively. In recent years the diffusion of small satellite dishes, especially in countries where the government attempts to control the media, has influenced political change.

III. Cultural Patterns and Processes

C. Cultural landscapes and cultural identity
3. Environmental impact of cultural attitudes and practices

The creation of uniform landscapes through the diffusion of popular culture can negatively impact the environment by depleting natural resources and polluting the landscape. Golf courses remake the environment as do some types of commercial agriculture, and the demand for some products puts a strain on natural resources. Popular cultures, such as fast-food generate more waste and thus lead to the pollution of the environment.

KEY TERMS

Built environment	Hearths
Cultural imperialism	Hierarchical diffusion
Custom	Indigenous architecture
Folk culture	Material culture
Folk housing	Popular culture
Folklore	Relocation diffusion
Folk songs	Taboo
Habit	Terroir

Key Issues Revisited

1. Where do folk and popular cultures originate and diffuse?
-as a result of distinctive processes of origin and diffusion, folk and popular cultures have different distribution patterns
-folk culture is more likely to have an anonymous origin and to diffuse slowly through migration
-popular culture is more likely to be invented and diffused rapidly with the use of modern communications

2. Why is folk culture clustered?
-unique folk cultures arise because of the lack of interaction among groups
-folk culture is more likely to be influenced by the local environment

3. Why is popular culture widely distributed?
-popular culture diffuses rapidly across the world, aided by modern communications, especially television
-differences in popular culture are more likely to be observed in one place at different points in time then among different places at one point in time

4. Why does globalization of popular culture cause problems?
-popular culture, usually originating in western MDCs, may cause the elimination of some folk culture
-popular culture may adversely affect the environment

Chapter 5: Language

      This chapter discusses language which, together with religion and ethnicity, is one of the three traits that best distinguishes cultural values. The chapter looks at where languages are spoken and why they have distinctive distributions. As well as addressing the globalization of English, the chapter also examines attempts to preserve local languages. The global distribution of languages results from a combination of interaction and isolation.

Key Issue 1 – Where are English-Language Speakers Distributed?

III. Cultural Patterns and Processes

A. Concepts of Culture
1. Traits
2. Diffusion

B. Cultural Differences
1. Language

      The English language became a distinct language in England as a result of westward Celtic migration, as well as the Germanic and Norman invasions. Modern English evolved mainly from the languages spoken by the German conquerors of Britain, the Angles, Saxons, and the Jutes (the word *England* comes from the *Angles'land*), and changed again with the arrival of the Normans in 1066. Modern English emerged from a mingling of French and Germanic. English diffused around the world during Britain's era of colonialism.

      Different dialects of a language develop through isolation from other speakers of the same language as well as by interaction with other speakers of that language. English has many dialects but **British Received Pronunciation (BRP)**, the dialect associated with upper-class Britons, is recognized as the **standard language** which is the most accepted dialect for mass communication. In France the Parisian dialect became the standard form of French.

III. Cultural Patterns and Processes

A. Concepts of culture
4. Cultural regions

      There are major dialect differences in English within Britain and the United States. Words that are associated with a dialect, such as the word that is used by children in Britain in a game of tag to signal that they have touched another participant, are spoken in a specific geographic region and thus have boundaries. This word-usage boundary is known as an **isogloss**.

Key Issue 2 – Why is English Related To Other Languages?

III. Cultural Patterns and Processes

A. Concepts of Culture
1. Traits

B. Cultural differences
1. Language

     Language is one of the oldest and most geographically diverse cultural traits on earth. It is a system of communication through speech. Many languages have a **literary tradition** although some have only an **oral tradition**.

     All languages belong to a **language family** which is a collection of many languages that were originally related through a common ancestor. The **Indo-European family** is the world's most spoken language family. A **language branch** is a collection of languages related through a common ancestor within a language family, although not as old. Germanic is one of the branches of the Indo-European language family. A **language group** is a set of languages within a branch that share a relatively recent common origin. English is a language in the West Germanic group of the Germanic group of the Indo-European family. **Dialects** are regionally distinct versions of a single language that are distinguished by vocabulary, spelling, and pronunciation. **Ebonics** is an African-American dialect in the United States. British and American English are examples of different dialects of English. Countries designate at least one language as their **official language**, which is used for all government business. A **monolingual state** will only have one official language that is used in this capacity. **Multilingual states,** such as Kenya (Swahili and English) and Switzerland (German, French, Italian and Romansh), have more than one official language. Belgium is a multilingual state because French and Flemish (a dialect of the Germanic language of Dutch) are both official languages, but the country has had more difficulty reconciling the interests of the different language speakers. **English** is known as a **lingua franca** because it is a language of international communication.

     Languages of the Indo-European family are spoken on all continents but are dominant in Europe and the Americas. There are eight branches of the Indo-European family. Large numbers of people speak a language of one of the following four branches: Indo-Iranian, Romance, Germanic, and Balto-Slavic.

     German and English are both part of the Germanic branch of Indo-European. The branch of Indo-European with the most speakers is Indo-Iranian which is divided into an eastern group (Indic), and a western group (Iranian). Hindi is the most spoken of the eastern group and Pakistan's principal language, Urdu, is essentially the same but written in the Arabic alphabet. The major Iranian group languages include Persian, Pashto, and Kurdish.

     The Balto-Slavic languages are largely those of Eastern Europe, especially Russian. The Romance languages, including Spanish, Portuguese, French, Italian, and Romanian, all developed from the Latin language of the Romans. Provincial people in the Roman Empire spoke a common form of Latin known as **Vulgar Latin**. Latin diffused with the expansion of the Roman republic and empire, and much later, during the era of Spanish and Portuguese imperialism in the Americas.

There are two theories about the origin and diffusion of Indo-European. The **Nomadic Warrior Thesis** or theory of Kurgan origin states that the first Indo-European speakers were Kurgans who lived near present-day Russia and Kazakhstan. They migrated westward into Europe, southward to Iran and South Asia, and eastward into Siberia, largely by military conquest. The theory of Anatolian origin states that the first speakers of Proto-Indo-European lived in eastern Anatolia two thousand years before the Kurgans, and that they migrated west into Europe and east into Asia with their agricultural practices, rather than by military conquest. Regardless of how Indo-European diffused, communication was poor and the result was isolation. Ultimately distinct languages evolved from distinct groups.

Key Issue 3 – Where Are Other Language Families Distributed?

III. Cultural Practices and Processes

A. Concepts of culture
1. Traits
4. Cultural regions

B. Cultural differences
1. Languages

The second largest language family is **Sino-Tibetan**, spoken by nearly twenty percent of the world's population. It includes most of Southeast Asia and China, which is the world's most populous state. The languages of China, of which Mandarin is the most important and widely spoken, generally belong to the Sinitic branch of the Sino-Tibetan family. Unlike Indo-European languages, Chinese languages are based on one-syllable words and have thousands of characters. Most of these characters are **ideograms**, which represent ideas or concepts rather than specific pronunciations. Other East and Southeast Asian language families include Japanese, Korean, Austro-Asiatic, and Austronesian. TaiKadai, once classified as a branch of the Sino-Tibetan family, is also an Asian language family, spoken in Thailand and neighboring portions of China. The major language families of the Middle East and Central Asia include Afro-Asiatic, Altaic, and Uralic (which was once classified with Altaic). More than ninety-five percent of the people in sub-Saharan Africa speak languages of the Niger-Congo, especially Swahili. Other African language families include Nilo-Saharan and Khoisan.

Key Issue 4 – Why do people preserve local languages?

III. Cultural Patterns and Processes

A. Concepts of culture
3. Acculturation, assimilation, and globalization

B. Cultural differences
1. Languages

Thousands of languages are **extinct languages**, once in existence but no longer in use today. The European language of Gothic is such an example. Languages can become extinct through the loss of an entire people or through linguistic evolution over time. However the pressures of economic and social **acculturation**, the **assimilation** of cultural traits such as language, by one group under the influence of another, are responsible for most of today's losses. Many African languages have become extinct because of the linguistic effects of European colonialism. Globalization today threatens many languages in the world.

III. Cultural Patterns and Processes

C. Cultural landscapes and cultural identity
1. Values and preferences
2. Symbolic landscapes and sense of place

Hebrew is a rare example of an extinct language that has been revived. The revival of this language is associated with the Zionist movement and the creation of the state of Israel in 1948. I t is one symbol of Israeli nationalism.
Endangered languages, such as those belonging to the Celtic branch of Indo-European, are experiencing a resurgence today. The revival of Irish Gaelic, Scottish Gaelic and Brythonic (Welsh) is linked to nationalistic movements in these parts of the British Isles. Other Celtic languages include Cornish and Breton.
When two groups of people with different languages meet, a new language with some characteristics of each may result so that they can communicate. This is called a **pidgin language**. Where the linguistic traditions of indigenous peoples and colonizers have blended, a **Creole language** will result. This has occurred in Louisiana and is one symbol of the distinctive culture that has developed in this region of the United States.
Languages develop and change as a result of diffusion and interaction among people. The widespread use of English in the French language is called **franglais**, and the diffusion of English into the Spanish language is called **Spanglish.Denglis h** is a combination of German and English. However some languages lack interaction with speakers of other languages. An **isolated language**, such as Basque in the Pyrenees Mountains, is one that is unrelated to any other language family.

KEY TERMS

Acculturation
Assimilation
British Received Pronunciation (BRP)
Creole or creolized language
Denglish
Dialect
Ebonics
Extinct Language
Franglais
Ideograms
Indo-European family
Isogloss
Isolated language
Language
Language branch

Language family
Language group
Lingua franca
Literary tradition
Monolingual country
Multilingual country
Nomadic Warrior Thesis
Official language
Oral tradition
Pidgin language
Sino-Tibetan family
Spanglish
Standard language
Vulgar Latin

Key Issues Revisited

1. Where are English-language speakers distributed?
-English can be traced to the invasions of England by Germanic tribes in the Dark Ages
-English diffused around the world from England as a result of colonialism
-Americans and English speak different dialects of English because of their relative isolation

2. Why is English related to other languages?
-English is part of the Germanic branch of the Indo-European language family
-nearly one-half of the world speak a language in the Indo-European family
-Indo-European languages developed from a single ancestor through migration, followed by isolation of one group from others

3. Where are other language families distributed?
-nearly one-fourth of the world speak a language in the Sino-Tibetan family
-a half-dozen other language families encompass another one-fourth of the world
-each language has a distinctive distribution, which is a result of a combination of migration and isolation

4. Why do people preserve local languages?
-English has become the most important language for international communication
-as a result of the global dominance of a lingua franca such as English, less widely used languages can become endangered or extinct
-some local languages are being preserved and revived because they are an important element of cultural identity

48

Chapter 6: Religion

The distribution and diffusion of major religions is outlined. The chapter also explains why certain religions have not diffused widely. The chapter goes on to discuss the relationship between religions and the physical environment. Finally religious conflict is addressed.

Key Issue 1 – Where are religions distributed?

III. Cultural Patterns and Processes

A. Concepts of culture
1. Traits

B. Cultural differences
2. Religion

As a cultural trait, **religion** helps to define people and how they understand the world around them. There are essentially two major types of religions, universalizing and ethnic. **Universalizing religions** appeal to people of many cultures, regardless of where they live in the world. Nearly 60% of the world's population adheres to a universalizing religion. **Ethnic religions** appeal primarily to one group of people living in one place. About 25% of the world's population follows an ethnic religion. Some religions are **monotheistic**, teaching the primacy of one god, whereas other religions are **polytheistic**, teaching that there are numerous gods. **Atheists** do not believe in any god.

Buddhism, Christianity, and Islam are the three major universalizing or **global religions**. Each is divided into branches, denominations, and sects. A **branch** is a fundamental division within a religion. A **denomination** is a division of a branch; this term is most commonly used to describe the Protestant denominations of Christianity. A **sect** is a group that is smaller than a denomination.

Buddhism is the oldest of the world's universalizing religions, with over 300 million adherents, mostly in China and Southeast Asia. Founded by Siddhartha Gautama in the 6th century B.C., Buddhism teaches that suffering originates from our attachment to life and other worldly possessions. The key concepts of Buddhism are outlined in the Four Noble Truths. Buddhism split into two main branches, Theravada and Mahayana, as followers disagreed on interpreting statements by Siddhartha Gautama. Theravada Buddhism is found in Southeast Asia, whereas Mahayana Buddhism is more prevalent in East Asia as well as Mongolia and Tibet. Unlike Christians and Muslims, most Buddhists also follow an ethnic religion too.

Christianity has about two billion adherents and is the world's most geographically widespread religion. Christians believe in one God and that his son, Jesus was the promised Messiah, delivering salvation to all people. Christianity has three major branches: Roman Catholic, Eastern Orthodox, and Protestant. The Roman Catholic Church, with its hearth at Vatican City in Rome, is the most important religion in large parts of Europe and North America, and is dominant in Latin America. Catholicism also exists on other continents. The Protestant Church began in the 1500's with Martin Luther's protests against the abuses of the Catholic Church. It is the most important religion in large parts of northern Europe as well as the regions of North America to which many people from northern Europe migrated. As with the Catholic Church, Protestantism also has adherents on other continents. The Eastern Orthodox branch of Christianity is only dominant in Eastern Europe and Russia, but also has adherents in smaller populations throughout the world.

Islam, with more than one million followers, is the dominant religion in North Africa and the Middle East, as well as Bangladesh and Indonesia. Islam is a monotheistic religion, based on the belief that there is one God, Allah, and that Mohammed was Allah's prophet. The word *Islam* in Arabic means *submission to the will of God*, and an adherent is a Muslim or *one who surrenders to God*. Islam is divided into two branches: *Sunni*, which is by far the larger of the two, and *Shiite*. In recent years there has been a rise in radical **fundamentalism** that has caused more division and conflict in the Muslim world. Most fundamentalists accept the holy book of Islam, the Koran, as the unquestioned guide on both religious and secular matters. Islamic fundamentalism avoids any sort of western influence and can contribute to intense conflict.

Sikhism and **Baha'i** are the two universalizing religions other than Buddhism, Christianity, and Islam with the largest umber of followers. Most Sikhs are located in the Punjab region of India, whereas Baha'is are dispersed among many countries, especially in Africa and Asia. **Mormonism** is a universalizing religion practiced in parts of the United States, especially Utah. As part of this religion, some of its adherents still practice **polygamy**, although this is now illegal in the United States.

Hinduism, with nearly 300 million adherents, is the largest ethnic religion and the world's third largest religion. Ethnic religions have much more clustered distributions than universalizing religions; the vast majority of Hindus live on the Indian subcontinent. For thousands of years Hindus in India have developed a unique society that integrates spiritual practices with daily life. Hindus believe that there is more than one path to reach God; there are thousands of deities in the Hindu belief system and thus the religion is polytheistic.

The other major ethnic religion is **Judaism** which was the first major monotheistic religion. Both Christianity and Judaism have some of their roots in Judaism; Jesus was born a Jew, and Mohammed traced his ancestry to Abraham. Judaism is based on a sense of ethnic identity in the lands bordering the eastern Mediterranean. Jewish people have been returning to this land since the end of the nineteenth century, and in 1948 the Jewish state of Israel was created. Today most Jews live in Israel and the United States.

Other ethnic religions include **Shintoism**, the ancient ethnic religion of Japan, which is still practiced today. **Confucianism** and **Daoism** (sometimes spelled Taoism) are sometimes distinguished as distinct ethnic religions in China, although many consider them to be philosophies more than ethnic religions. There is a lot of mixing of these philosophies and religions. Some Africans still practice **animism**, or traditional ethnic religions, although there has been a rapid decline in African animism because of the increase in the numbers of Christians and Muslims.

Key Issue 2 – Why do religions have different distributions?

III. Cultural Patterns and Processes

A. Concepts of culture
2. Diffusion

B. Cultural differences
2. Religion

The three universalizing religions diffused from **hearths**, or places of origin that are associated with the lives of their founders. Christianity diffused through relocation diffusion where **missionaries** carried the teachings of Jesus around the Mediterranean world. Expansion diffusion was also important as **pagans**, followers of ancient polytheistic religions, were converted to Christianity. It diffused beyond the European realm during the age of colonialism beginning in the early 1500's.

Islam diffused from its hearth at Mecca through military conquest across North Africa, Southern Europe and other parts of Southwest Asia. Arab traders brought the religion to sub-Saharan Africa and later Indonesia.

Buddhism diffused from its hearth in northern India to the island of Ceylon (present day Sri Lanka) and eastwards into East and Southeast Asia as a result of missionary activity and trade.

III. Cultural Patterns and Processes

A. Concepts of culture
3. Acculturation, assimilation, and globalization

Universalizing religions have supplanted and mingled with ethnic religions in various parts of the world. In some parts of Africa that were colonized by Europeans, Christianity has replaced animistic religions. In other parts of the continent the two have merged. In East Asia, especially Japan, Buddhism and Shintoism have merged.

III. Cultural Patterns and Processes

A. Concepts of culture
4. Cultural regions

Since Roman times Jews have been forced to leave the eastern Mediterranean and disperse throughout the world, an action known as the **diaspora** (from the Greek word for *dispersion*). Historically Jews were persecuted and forced to live in **ghettos**, city areas set up by law to be inhabited only by Jews, in many European countries. Since the Nazi Holocaust many Jews have returned to the Middle East and today Israel is a Jewish state, although Judaism, unlike other ethnic religions, is practiced in many countries.

III. Cultural Patterns and Processes

C. Cultural landscapes and cultural identity
1. Values and preferences
2. Symbolic landscapes and sense of place

Both universalizing and ethnic religions have holy places that are usually associated with the history of that religion. Adherents will make a religions journey or **pilgrimage** to holy places.

Buddhist holy places or shrines mark the location of important events in Buddha's life and are in northern India and southern Nepal. The holiest locations in Islam are associated with the life of Mohammed, and include in order of importance, Makkah (Mecca), Madinah (Medina), and Jerusalem. Holy places in ethnic religions are closely tied to physical geography. For example, to Hindus the River Ganges is the holiest river in India and they believe that bathing in its waters will achieve purification.

Universalizing and ethnic religions have a different understanding of the relationship between people and their environment. This is exemplified in their different attitudes towards **cosmogony**, the set of religious beliefs that concern the origin of the universe, and the calendar, which for ethnic religions is very much tied to physical geography. The **solstice** has special significance in some ethnic religions and has its origins in some pagan religions.

Key Issue 3 – Why do religions organize space in distinctive patterns?

III. Cultural Patterns and Processes

A. Concepts of culture
4. Cultural regions

B. Cultural differences
2. Religion

The Roman Catholic Church is a good example of a **hierarchical religion**, with its well-defined geographical structure and division of territory into local administrative units. Archbishops report to the Pope and each heads a **province**. Bishops report to archbishops and administer a **diocese**, which is the basic unit of the geographic organization of the Roman Catholic Church. The headquarters of a bishop is called a *see* and is usually the largest city in the diocese. A priest reports to a bishop and heads a **parish**.

Islam and some Protestant denominations are good examples of **autonomous religions** because they are relatively self-sufficient with little interaction between communities within the religion.

III. Cultural Patterns and Processes

C. Cultural landscapes and cultural identity
1. Values and preferences
2. Symbolic landscapes and sense of place

Religion impacts the landscape in a variety of ways. Christian churches were originally modeled after Roman basilicas. Mosques are the most important religious buildings in the Islamic world, and they also serve as places for the community to gather. Most Hindus worship at home although Hindu temples serve as shrines to one or more of their gods. The pagoda is the most visible religious architecture of the Buddhist and Shintoist landscape, and contains the relics of Buddhism.

Burial practices of different religions are also visible on the landscape. Christians, Muslims, and Jews usually bury their dead in cemeteries.

Place names or toponyms also show the impact of religion on the landscape. For example many Roman Catholic places are named for saints. Religious buildings, places of pilgrimage, burial locations, and place names are all examples of **sacred spaces**.

III. Cultural Patterns and Processes

C. Cultural landscapes and cultural identity
3. Environmental impact of cultural attitudes and practices

Cremation has replaced burial as a means of disposing of the dead in many parts of the world because of the pressure on agricultural land. This is particularly true in China and Western Europe. Cremation is also used in the Hindu world although it is putting an increasing strain on India's wood supplies.

Key Issue 4 – Why do territorial conflicts arise among religious groups?

III. Cultural Patterns and Processes

B. Cultural differences
2. Religion
3. Ethnicity

Religious identification can lead to religious conflict. The Hindu **caste system**, which was the hereditary class into which a Hindu was placed according to religious law, has led to social and ethnic conflict in India. These issues are less significant now that the caste system has been legally abolished. The rise of communism has also been a challenge to organized religion, especially in Eastern Europe and Asia.

Religious conflict continues in many parts of the world especially at the boundaries between different religions, branches, and denominations. These conflicts have complex historical, social, and ethnic roots and must be also understood in the context of political geography. For example there has been longstanding conflict in the

Middle East. The city of Jerusalem contains sites that are sacred to Judaism, Christianity, and Islam. There have been religious wars in Ireland between Catholics and Protestants that have their origins in the English conquest of Ireland centuries ago. Tibetan Buddhism has been undermined by Chinese Communism since the latter's takeover of Tibet in 1950. There is concern that many Tibetan Buddhist traditions will be lost forever when the Dalai Lama and present generation of priests die.

KEY TERMS

Animism	**Hinduism**
Atheism	**Islam**
Autonomous religions	**Judaism**
Baha'i	**Missionary**
Branch	**Monotheism**
Buddhism	**Pagan**
Caste system	**Parish**
Christianity	**Pilgrimage**
Confucianism	**Polygamy**
Cosmogony	**Polytheism**
Daoism	**Province**
Denomination	**Religion**
Diaspora	**Sacred Spaces**
Diocese	**Sect**
Ethnic religion	**Shintoism**
Fundamentalism	
Ghetto	**Sikhism**
Global religions	**Solstice**
Hearth	**Universalizing religion**
Hierarchical religion	

Key Issues Revisited

1. Where are religions distributed?
-the world has three large universalizing religions – Christianity, Islam, and Buddhism – each with their own distinctive distribution
-Hinduism is the largest ethnic religion, and most of its adherents are clustered in India

2. Why do religions have different distributions?
-universalizing religions have a known origin and clear pattern of diffusion
-ethnic religions usually have unknown origins and little diffusion
-holy places and holidays in a universalizing religion are related to events in the life of its founder or prophet
-holy places and holidays in an ethnic religion are related to the local physical geography

3. Why do religions organize space in distinctive patterns?
-some religions have elaborate places of worship
-religions affect the landscape in other ways too, including the building of religious communities, toponyms marking the landscape, and land reserved for burying the dead
-some universalizing religions organize their territory into a rigid administrative structure

4. Why do territorial conflicts arise among religions groups?
-expansion of the territory occupied by one religion may reduce the territory of another
-religions must compete for control of territory with nonreligious ideas, such as economic modernization

Chapter 7: Ethnicity

The geographic distribution of ethnicities is initially considered in this chapter. Ethnic groups are tied to particular places because members of the group, or their ancestors, were born or raised there. Another important consideration here is ethnic conflict in specific areas of the world. The attempt to retain distinct ethnic identity is one example of the preservation of local diversity.

Key Issue 1 – Where are ethnicities distributed?

III. Cultural Patterns and Processes

A. Concepts of culture
1. Traits

B. Cultural differences
3. Ethnicity

Ethnicity comes from the Greek root *ethnos* which means *national*. Ethnicity is identity with a group of people who share a common identity with a specific homeland or hearth. It is distinct from **race** which is identity with a group of people who share a biological ancestor. Biological classification by race is the basis for **racism**, which is the belief that racial differences produce an inherent superiority of a particular race. A **racist** is someone who follows the beliefs of racism. The characteristics of ethnicity derive from the distinctive features of specific geographic locations whereas those of race are not rooted in particular places.

The two most numerous ethnicities in the United States are Hispanics (or Latinos), at 15% of total population, and African Americans at 13%. About 4% are Asian-America and 1% American Indian. At a regional scale African-Americans are clustered in the Southeast, Hispanics in the Southwest, Asian-Americans in the West, and American Indians in the Southwest and Plains states. At the urban level African-Americans and Hispanics are highly clustered in **ethnic neighborhoods**, especially in northern cities. At the same time these cities are also **multicultural**.

Discrimination by race was the cornerstone of the South African legal system of apartheid. **Apartheid** was the physical separation of different races into separate geographic areas. It was instituted by the white racist Afrikaners government in 1948, and was particularly designed to subjugate the black majority by forcing them to live in impoverished homelands. The apartheid laws were repealed in the 1990's, but although South Africa now has black majority rule, it will take many years to redress their geographic impact.

III. Cultural Patterns and Processes

A. Concepts of culture
2. Diffusion

Three major migration patterns have shaped the present distribution of African-Americans within the United States. The first was the forced migration from Africa that was part of the **triangular slave trade**. After slavery most African-Americans remained in the rural South working as **sharecroppers**, farming land rented from a landowner and paying rent in the form of crops. Blacks were still separated from whites in the South through laws that followed the Supreme Court's "separate but equal" treatment of the races. The second major migration pattern was the migration to Northern cities from the beginning of the twentieth century. In these cities, African-American immigrants lived in **ghettos**, named for the term for neighborhoods where Jews were forced to live in medieval Europe. Segregation laws were eliminated during the 1950's and 1960's. The third migration pattern was their movement from ghettos into neighborhoods immediately adjacent during this time. This was made possible by "white flight" to the suburbs which in turn was encouraged by **blockbusting**, where real estate agents convinced white homeowners living near a black area to sell their houses at low prices.

Key Issue 2 – Why have ethnicities been transformed into nationalities?

III. Cultural Patterns and Processes

A. Concepts of culture
1. Traits
4. Cultural regions

B. Cultural differences
3. Ethnicity

IV. Political Organization of Space

A. Territorial dimensions of politics
5. Spatial relationships between political patterns and patterns of ethnicity, economy, and environment

C. Changes and challenges to political-territorial arrangements
1. Changing nature of sovereignty
2. Fragmentation, unification, alliance

Nationality, which comes from the Latin word *nasci*, meaning *to have been born*, is identity with a group of people who share legal attachment and personal allegiance to a country. The desire for self-rule or **self-determination** has transformed ethnic groups into nationalities. A **nation-state** is a state whose territory corresponds to that occupied by a particular ethnicity. There are numerous nation-states in Europe including France, Slovenia, and Denmark. However no nation-state consists entirely of people from the same ethnic group. For example there are some German speakers in Denmark, and some Danish speakers in Germany.

Nationalism refers to the degree of loyalty that one has for a nationality. This could be instilled by promoting symbols of nationalism such as flags and songs. Nationalism is an example of a **centripetal force**, which is one that tends to unify people behind the state. **Centrifugal forces** do exactly the opposite and may lead to the breakup of a state.

      Multi-ethnic states contain more than one dominant ethnicity. For example Belgium is divided among the Dutch-speaking Flemish and the French-speaking Walloons. They are also called **multi-national states**, and each ethnic group will generally recognize each other as distinct nationalities. This is true of the United Kingdom today with its four major nationalities – English, Welsh, Scottish, and (northern) Irish. All four field their own national soccer teams. The former Soviet Union was the largest multinational state with fifteen republics that represented many different ethnic groups. Now they are independent states in the Baltic, Eastern Europe, Central Asia, and the Caucasus. There are geopolitical problems in the Caucasus because the boundaries of Armenia, Azerbaijan, and Georgia do not completely match the territories occupied by these ethnicities. For example there are minorities of Armenians in Azerbaijan and vice versa. Russia is still the largest multinational state with 39 nationalities, many of which, like Chechnya, want to be independent.

      There has been a resurgence of ethnic identity and nationalism in Eastern Europe since the 1980's. Prior to the 1980's this was effectively suppressed by Communist control. This has led to the breakup of the Soviet Union, Yugoslavia, and Czechoslovakia, and the emergence of smaller nation-states. Slovenia is a good example of a nation-state that emerged from the former Yugoslavia in the 1990's. Slovenes comprise more than 90% of the population of Slovenia; thus the country is relatively peaceful and stable. These movements for **self-determination** are fueled by **ethnonationalism**, a strong feeling of belonging to a nation that is a minority within a state.

Key Issue 3 – Why do ethnicities clash?

III. Cultural Patterns and Processes

B. Cultural differences
3. Ethnicity

IV. Political Organization of Space

A. Territorial dimensions of politics
5. Spatial relationships between political patterns and patterns of ethnicity, economy, and environment

      In some countries ethnicities within a state will compete to dominate the national identity of that state. This will often result in civil war. This has been the case in a number of countries in the Horn of Africa. Eritrean rebels fought against the Ethiopian army in the early 1990's and became the independent state of Eritrea in 1993. There has been conflict between the two over the location of the border since that time. There has been civil war in Sudan for decades between the Christian and animist rebels in the south and the Arab-Muslim dominated government forces in the north. Now there is ethnic war in the western-most Darfur region. Somalia is a country in turmoil because of conflict between the six major ethnic groups, known as clans.

In the Middle East Lebanon has experienced civil war because of ethnic and religious divisions. The country is comprised of numerous Christian sects as well as Muslims belonging to both the Shiite and Sunni sects. The island country of Sri Lanka has been torn by fighting between the Sinhalese Buddhists who speak an Indo-European language, and the Tamil Hindus who speak a Dravidian language. The long war between the ethnicities ended in 2009 with the defeat of the Tamil.

Conflicts also arise when one ethnicity is split among more than one country. For example there have been major ethnic disputes between India and Pakistan since these countries became independent from Britain in 1947. Even though there was massive forced migration at the time of independence, there are still minorities of Hindus in Pakistan and minorities of Muslims in India. In addition, the two countries never agreed on the location of their boundary in the northern region of Kashmir.

Key Issue 4 – What is ethnic cleansing?

III. Cultural Patterns and Processes

B. Cultural differences
3. Ethnicity

IV. Political Organization of Space

A. Territorial dimensions of politics
5. Spatial relationships between political patterns and patterns of ethnicity, economy, and environment

Throughout history conflict between ethnic groups has led to forced migration. **Ethnic cleansing** is the process by which a more powerful ethnic group forcibly removes a less powerful one in order to create their own nation or nation-state. The case of ethnic cleansing in Bosnia and Herzegovina is a classic recent example. Bosnia was the most multi-ethnic republic of former Yugoslavia. At the time of the breakup of Yugoslavia in the early 1990's the population of Bosnia consisted of 48% Bosnian Muslim, 37% Serb, and 14% Croat. Serbs and Croats fought to unite their ethnicity in Bosnia with their respective republics; this is called **irredentism**. The Serbs in Bosnia were **irredenta** of Serbia. To do this they both engaged in ethnic cleansing of Bosnian Muslims.

After the breakup of Yugoslavia, Serbia remained a multi-ethnic state. In fact their southern **province** of Kosovo is 90% ethnic Albanian. Serbia launched a campaign of ethnic cleansing of the Albanian majority. Eventually Serbia withdrew its troops from Kosovo as a result of a North Atlantic Treaty Organization (NATO) air attack. Kosovo declared its independence from Serbia in 2008.

The Balkans has always been a region of ethnic conflict. Indeed the term **balkanized** is used to describe a geographic area that cannot be organized into one or more stable states. **Balkanization** is the process by which a state breaks down through ethnic conflict. The region is also referred to as a **shatterbelt** for the same reasons.

Ethnic cleansing led to **genocide** in Rwanda in the 1990's because of long-standing conflict between the Hutus and the Tutsis. The Hutus were farmers and the Tutsis were cattle herders. Historically the Tutsi took control and made the Hutus their

60

serfs. The region was colonized by the Belgians and Germans and, shortly before independence in 1962 Hutus killed or ethnically cleansed most of the Tutsis. The 1994 ethnic cleansing and genocide was when Tutsis defeated the Hutu army and killed half a million Hutus. This conflict has spilled into neighboring countries, especially the Democratic Republic of the Congo, and the region is still very unstable because of ethnic conflict.

KEY TERMS

Apartheid
Balkanization
Balkanized
Blockbusting
Centripetal forces
Centrifugal forces
Ethnic cleansing
Ethnic neighborhoods
Ethnicity
Ethnonationalism
Genocide
Ghettos
Irredenta
Irredentism

Multicultural
Multi-ethnic state
Multinational state
Nationalism
Nationality
Nation-state
Province
Race
Racism
Racist
Self-determination
Sharecropper
Shatterbelt
Triangular slave trade

Key Issues Revisited

1. Where are ethnicities distributed?
-major ethnicities in the United States include African Americans, Hispanic Americans, and Asian Americans
-these ethnic groups are clustered in regions of the country and within urban areas
-sometimes race and ethnicity are used interchangeably

2. Why have ethnicities been transformed into nationalities?
-nationalities are ethnic groups that are attached and loyal to a particular country
-nationality combines an ethnic group's language, religion, history, and other patriotic events
-many countries have been created in an attempt to transform single ethnic groups into single nationalities

3. Why do ethnicities clash?
-conflicts can develop when a country contains several ethnicities that vie for political control
-conflicts can also develop when an ethnicity is divided among more than one country

4. What is ethnic cleansing?

-ethnic cleansing is an attempt by one ethnic group to remove all members of another ethnic group in order to create an ethnically homogeneous region

-ethnic cleansing was practiced in the conflict in Yugoslavia during the 1990's

Chapter 8: Political Geography

This chapter outlines the location of states and the changing face of **geopolitics** since the end of the Cold War. The location of boundaries gives some indication as to potential instability and boundary disputes between countries. States also cooperate with each other, and some countries have transferred military, economic, and political authority to regional and worldwide collections of states. Finally the chapter considers reasons for terrorist attacks, and the relationship between terrorism and political geography.

Key Issue 1 – Where are states located?

IV. Political Organization of Space

A. Territorial dimensions of politics
1. The concept of territoriality

The concept of dividing the world into a collection of independent states is relatively recent, dating from 18th century Europe, but the concept of territoriality can be traced to the ancient Middle East. The first states in Mesopotamia, which was at the eastern end of the ancient Fertile Crescent, were known as city-states. A **city-state** is a sovereign state that consists of a town or city and the surrounding countryside.

Later the Roman Empire provided the best example of the power of political unity. After the collapse of the Roman Empire in the fifth century A.D. Europe was divided into a large number of feudal estates. Ultimately powerful kings gained control in Western Europe and their kingdoms formed the basis for the development of the modern states that included England, France, and Spain.

IV. Political Organization of Space

B. Evolution of the contemporary political pattern
1. The nation-state concept

Political geography can be studied at a number of different scales, including local, national, and international politics. The fundamental unit of political geography is the country which is formally called a **state**. This is an area organized into a political unit and ruled by an established government that has **sovereignty** over its internal and external affairs. This definition if a state is tested in some places, notably Korea, China and Taiwan, Western Sahara (Sahrawi Republic), and the polar regions. North and South Korea were admitted to the United Nations as separate countries but they both have some commitment to reunification. China has claimed Taiwan since the establishment of that country when Nationalists fled there from China in the late 1940's. Morocco still claims Western Sahara although most African countries recognize it as a sovereign state. The polar regions are the only large landmasses on the Earth's surface that are not part of a state. Antarctica is managed by the Antarctic Treaty (1959) which allows states to establish research stations on the continent. The United Nations Convention on the Law of the Sea (1982) has allowed states to submit claims within the Arctic Circle.

A **nation** consists of a group of people with a common ethnic and political identity, but every nation does not have its own state. A **nation-state** is where political boundaries coincide with the territory occupied by a particular ethnicity that has been transformed into a nationality.

The land area occupied by states varies considerably in the world. Russia is the largest state, encompassing 11% of the world's land area. Other large states include China, Canada, the United States, and Brazil. There are also numerous very small states or **microstates**. States such as Monaco and Vatican City, both of which are located within Italy, are good examples of microstates. Larger states usually have more extensive natural resources.

At the international geopolitical level three theories have been important in the development of the nation-state concept in the last two hundred years. In the late nineteenth century Friedrich Ratzel proposed his **organic theory** of the evolution of nations. According to Ratzel, states that did not expand their land area would disintegrate like an organism that fails to find food. Sir Halford Mackinder developed his **heartland theory** at the beginning of the twentieth century. He believed that the Eurasian landmass was the world's heartland and thus the key to world domination. Nicholas Spykman disagreed, and argued the rimland area surrounding the heartland and including the world's oceans was the key to world political power; this was his **rimland theory.**

IV. Political Organization of Space

B. Evolution of the contemporary political pattern
2. Colonialism and Imperialism

European states controlled much of the world through **colonialism** beginning in the early 1500's. They established **colonies** by imposing their political, economic, and cultural control (especially religion) on territories in Latin America, Asia, and Africa that became legally tied to them. Some states that remained independent became **buffer states** separating areas of colonial control. For example, Thailand became a buffer state between British India and French Indochina. Technically colonialism refers to the control of territory previously uninhabited whereas **imperialism** is the control of territory that is already occupied, but the two terms are used interchangeably.

Latin American countries became independent in the first half of the nineteenth century, and **decolonization** proceeded rapidly across Africa and Asia after World War Two. Today there are only a few remaining colonies and these are generally only very small territories around the globe.

Key Issue 2 – Where do boundaries between states cause problems?

IV. Political Organization of Space

A. Territorial dimensions of politics
3. Influences of boundaries on identity, interaction, and exchange

State (or territorial) morphology, or the shape of a state determines the length of its boundaries with other states, as well as potential communication and conflict with neighboring states.

Countries like Poland that are relatively rounded are **compact states**. This shape enhances communications between all regions especially when the capital is centrally located.

Prorupted states are compact states with a large projecting extension. Proruptions can disrupt, like the Afghanistan proruption which denies Russia a shared boundary with Pakistan. They can also provide access such as Namibia's proruption which was originally designed to give this former German colony access to the Zambezi River in south-west Africa.

Elongated states, such as Chile and The Gambia, are long and thin. Such states often suffer from poor internal communications.

A state that is divided into several discontinuous pieces of territory is called a **fragmented state**. The United States is fragmented because Alaska is separated from the contiguous lower forty-eight states. Kaliningrad is separated from the rest of Russia by the independent states of Lithuania and Belarus. Island states like Indonesia are fragmented because of water. In addition some states have fragmented territory that lies completely within the boundary of another state. This was the case with West Berlin during the Cold War and is called an **exclave**. The boundary between East and West Berlin as well as the boundary between East and West Germany is now a **relic boundary** because it no longer exists. An **enclave** is a piece of territory that is surrounded by another political unit of which it is not a part. Lesotho is an enclave because it is completely surrounded by South Africa.

States like Italy and South Africa that completely surround other states are known as **perforated states**. The states that are completely surrounded, such as Lesotho by South Africa, are also **landlocked states** that lack access to the ocean or sea.

The various shapes of states provide both advantages and disadvantages. Some states occupy strategically important locations on the earth's surface. This is true of Singapore on the tip of Malaysia in South-East Asia, and Panama on the isthmus between North and South America.

IV. Political Organization of Space

A. Territorial dimensions of politics
2. The nature and meaning of boundaries

States are separated from each other by borders, called **boundaries**. A boundary is an invisible line that completely surrounds a state, marks the outer limits of its territorial control, and gives it a distinctive shape. Prior to the establishment of formal boundaries, **frontiers** separated states. A frontier is a zone or area between states where no state exercises complete control. Frontiers do still exist between states on the Arabian Peninsula where the borders are virtually uninhabited desert regions.

Physical boundaries follow important physical features on the landscape, such as water, mountains, and deserts. For example the boundary between France and Spain is the crest of the Pyrenees Mountains, and boundary separating Uganda, Kenya, and

Tanzania runs through Lake Victoria. Physical boundaries are often **antecedent boundaries** because they were natural boundaries long before those areas became populated.

There are a number of different types of **cultural boundaries** between states. **Geometric boundaries** follow straight lines and have little to do with the physical or cultural landscape. The boundaries between many African states today are geometric. They are also called **superimposed boundaries** because they were drawn by European colonial powers that did not pay any attention to the social, cultural or ethnic compositions of African people.

When British India became independent in 1948 the boundary that was created between the newly independent states of India and Pakistan was essentially a **religious boundary**. It separated a predominantly Muslim Pakistan from a predominantly Hindu India. It is also a superimposed boundary in that it was drawn long after the area had been settled had established itself.

Language boundaries have always been important cultural boundaries between ethnic groups. This has been especially true in Western Europe for centuries and is becoming increasingly important in Southern and Eastern Europe.

There are now accepted **maritime boundaries** in the world's oceans. As a result of the **United Nations Convention on the Law of the Sea (UNCLOS)**, each state with an ocean boundary has a twelve mile **territorial sea**, and a two hundred mile **Exclusive Economic Zone (EEZ)** over which it has certain economic rights. Where the water distance between two countries is less than 24 miles, sometimes called **choke points**, **median lines** delimit the boundary between the two countries equidistant from each shore. **Delimitation** refers to the actual creation of a boundary as a cartographic representation. Beyond this two hundred mile limit lie the **high seas** that are beyond national jurisdiction, and are free and open for all countries to use.

IV. Political Organization of Space

A. Territorial dimensions of politics
5. Spatial relationships between political patterns and patterns of ethnicity, economy, and environment

C. Changes and challenges to political-territorial arrangements
2. Fragmentation, unification, alliance
3. Supranationalism and devolution

Territorial conflict often occurs if a state contains more than one ethnic group. A **multinational state** contains two or more ethnic groups. The island of Cyprus contains two ethnic groups, Greek and Turkish. The two nationalities are geographically separated on the island by a **demarcation** zone created by the United Nations. The former Soviet Union was the largest multinational state in the world, and contained fifteen republics that are now independent states. Russia is still the largest multinational state because there are still ethnic groups within Russia, like Chechnya that are fighting for **self-determination** or the right to become an independent state. Thus in spite of greater global political cooperation, local diversity has increased in political affairs and individual ethnic groups are demanding more control over territory. The pressures for independence within a multinational state from various ethnic groups are also known as **devolution** or **devolutionary pressures**. These pressures are also referred to as **centrifugal forces** because they pull countries apart.

Conflict can also occur where an ethnic group is divided among more than one state. In the Caucasus region there are minorities of Armenia in Azerbaijan and vice versa. The Kurds are a **stateless** ethnic group split among these two states as well as four others in the region.

Political geographers have identified four major types of boundary disputes between states. **Definitional boundary disputes** are over the legal language of a boundary agreement. **Locational boundary disputes** focus on issues related to the delimitation and demarcation of the boundary. **Operational boundary disputes** are conflicts dealing with the operation or functioning of a boundary, and **allocational boundary disputes** are usually over conflicts about resources at the boundary, especially where the boundary is at sea.

IV. Political Organization of Space

A. Territorial dimensions of politics
4. Federal and unitary states

B. Evolution of the contemporary political pattern
3. Democratization

The governments of states are generally organized in one of two ways. **Unitary states** place most power in the hands of the central government and work best in relatively small nation-states. The best examples of unitary states are those of Western Europe such as Britain and France. **Centripetal forces**, such as the reliance on a strong central government, strong national institutions, and a sense of common history, bind countries together.

Federal states allocate significant power to the units of local government and work well in multinational states where there is potential ethnic conflict. The United States is a federal state, not so much because of ethnic conflict but because of its sheer geographic size. In recent years there has been a global trend toward federal government. Both France and Poland have moved from a unitary toward a federal system in the last few years.

IV. Political Organization of Space

B. Evolution of the contemporary political pattern
3. Democratization

C. Changes and challenges to political-territorial arrangements
4. Electoral geography, including gerrymandering

The boundaries separating legislative districts in the United States and other countries have to be redrawn from time to time in order to account for changing population. For example the districts of the 435 U.S. House of Representatives are redrawn after the census every ten years. This is called **reapportionment** or **redistricting**. In most U.S. states this is done by the state legislature and historically the political party in control has tried to do this. The redrawing of legislative boundaries to benefit a specific political party in power is called **gerrymandering**. The term was named for Elbridge Gerry, a nineteenth century politician from Massachusetts who tried to do this in his state, and created an oddly shaped district that looked like a salamander that his opponents called a "gerrymander."

There are three types of gerrymandering. "Wasted votes" spreads opposition supporters across many districts. "Excess vote" concentrates opposition in few districts, and "Stacked vote" links distant areas of similar voters through oddly shaped boundaries. Although the Supreme Court has ruled gerrymandering illegal, stacked vote gerrymandering is still a reality.

Key Issue 3 – Why do states cooperate with each other?

IV. Political Organization of Space

B. Evolution of the contemporary political pattern
3. Democratization

C. Changes and challenges to political-territorial arrangements
2. Fragmentation, unification, alliance
3. Supranationalism and devolution

One of the most important trends in international politics is the development of international and regional alliances. **International organizations** are alliances of two or more countries seeking cooperation. The **United Nations** (UN) and the **North American Free Trade Agreement** (NAFTA) are both examples of international alliances. The UN is a global organization that focuses on peace and security whereas NAFTA is a regional economic alliance. The **European Union** (EU) is also a regional economic union but it also includes elements of political unity. All of these organizations are **supranational organizations** that include the membership of two or more states that relinquish some degree of sovereignty for the benefits of an alliance with other states.

When a large number of states were of roughly equal strength, no single state could dominate. This was the geopolitical situation in Europe before the First World War where European states formed opposing alliances and a **balance of power** was maintained. This changed after the Second World War when the **Warsaw Pact** and the **North Atlantic Treaty Organization** (NATO) became the opposing military alliances of the Cold War. Balance of power became bipolar. Most East European countries were controlled by the Soviet Union during the Cold War and were known as **satellite states**. **Confederations** are similar to international organizations in that they bring several states together for a common purpose. The **Commonwealth of Independent States** (CIS), a confederacy of independent states of the former Soviet Union for common economic and administrative needs, is an example if such an alliance. There are numerous other regional organizations in the world that combine political, military, and economic goals. Other prominent regional organizations include the **Organization on Security and**

Cooperation in Europe (OSCE), the **Organization of American States** (OAS), the **African Union** (AU), and the **Commonwealth**.

Key Issue 4 – Why has terrorism increased?

IV. Political Organization of Space

C. Changes and challenges to political-territorial arrangements
5. Terrorism

Terrorism is the systematic use of violence by a group in order to intimidate a population or coerce a government into granting its demands. It is sometimes hard to distinguish terrorism from other acts of political violence. This is the case with some of the actions of the Palestinians against Israel, and Chesham rebels against Russia.

There have been a number of terrorist attacks against the United States in recent years but the most dramatic and devastating was on September 11, 2001. Al-Qaeda has been implicated in many of these attacks including the September 11, 2001 attack. Founded by Osama bin Laden, al-Qaeda consists of numerous cells, unites *jihad* fighters, and has used fundamentalist Islam to justify attacks, especially against the United States.

Several states in the Middle East have also provided support for terrorism at three levels. Some have provided sanctuary for terrorists wanted by other countries. They have supplied weapons, money, and intelligence to terrorists, and some countries have planned attacks using terrorists. These countries have included Libya, Afghanistan, Iraq, and Iran at various times in recent years.

KEY TERMS

African Union (AU)
Allocational boundary disputes
Antecedent boundaries
Balance of power
Boundary
Buffer state
Centrifugal forces
Centripetal forces
Choke point
City-state
Colonialism
Colonies
Commonwealth
Commonwealth of Independent States (CIS)
Compact state

Confederation
Cultural boundaries
Decolonization
Definitional boundary disputes
Delimitation
Demarcation
Devolution
Elongated state
Enclave
European Union (EU)
Exclave
Exclusive Economic Zone (EEZ)
Federal states
Fragmented state
Frontier
Geometric boundaries

Geopolitics
Gerrymandering
Heartland theory
High seas
Imperialism
International organizations
Landlocked
Locational boundary disputes
Maritime boundaries
Median lines
Microstates
Multinational state
Nation
Nation-state
North American Free Trade
Association (NAFTA)
North Atlantic Treaty Organization
(NATO)
Operational boundary disputes
Organic theory
Organization of American States
(OAS)
Organization on Security and
Cooperation in Europe (OSCE)

Perforated state
Physical boundaries
Prorupted state
Reapportionment
Redistricting
Relic boundary
Religious boundaries
Rimland theory
Satellite states
Self-determination
Sovereignty
State
Stateless
State morphology
Subsequent boundaries
Superimposed boundaries
Supranational organizations
Territorial sea
Terrorism
Unitary state
United Nations (UN)
United Nations Convention on the
Law of the Sea (UNCLOS)
Warsaw Pact

Key Issues Revisited

1. Where are states located?
-a state is a political unit, with an organized government and sovereignty
-a nation is a group of people with a strong sense of cultural unity
-most of the Earth's surface is allocated to states, and only a few colonies and areas of unorganized territory remain

2. Why do boundaries between states cause problems?
-usually boundaries are drawn to coincide with physical features, such as mountains deserts, and bodies of water, or with cultural characteristics such as geometry, religion, and language
-boundaries affect the shape of countries and affect the ability of a country to live peacefully with its neighbors
-problems arise when the boundaries of states do not coincide with the boundaries of ethnicities

3. Why do states cooperate with each other?
-after the Second World War, the United States and the Soviet Union, the world's two superpowers, formed military alliances with other countries

-now that the Cold War has ended, nationalities are cooperating with each other, especially in western Europe, primarily to promote economic growth rather than to provide military protection

4. Why has terrorism increased?
-terrorism initiated by individuals, organizations, and states has increased, especially against the United States
-terrorists consider all U.S. citizens justified targets because they believe that all U.S. citizens are responsible for U.S. government policies and cultural practices

Chapter 9: Development

The chapter identifies the location of more and less developed countries and then explains why some regions are more developed than others. Obviously less developed countries face much greater obstacles to development. More and less developed regions are distinguished by economic, social, and demographic indicators. Level of development varies according to gender.

Key Issue 1 – Why does development vary among countries?

VI. Industrialization and Economic Development

B. Contemporary patterns and impacts of industrialization and development
2. Variations in levels of development

The United Nations HDI identifies gross domestic product per capita (GDP) as its economic indicator of development. Other economic indicators that help to distinguish between levels of development include economic structure, worker productivity, access to raw materials and availability of consumer goods. GDP is the value of all goods and services produced in a country, usually in a year. The annual per capita GDP in 2008 exceeded $30,000 in developed countries, and was from about $1,000 to $4,000 in developing countries and this gap has been widening. It is not a perfect measure of economic development because people in many developing countries still operate in largely non-monetary economies, and it measures average wealth rather than distribution.

The percentage of workers in the different sectors of the economy will help to show the level of development of a country. Workers in the **primary sector** of the economy extract materials from the Earth, usually through agriculture. The share of GDP accounted for by the primary sector has decreased in LDCs, but it remains higher than in MDCs. The **secondary sector** is the industrial sector of the economy, and the **tertiary sector** is the service sector of the economy; in MDC's, employment in the secondary sector has decreased. The share of GDP accounted for by the tertiary sector is relatively large in MDCs. Quaternary sector jobs include business services and wholesaling, and quinary sector jobs are in health, education, research, government, retailing, and tourism. However the current practice is to consider all these jobs as groups within the tertiary sector.

Productivity is the value of a particular product compared to the amount of labor needed to make it. It can be measured by the **value added** per worker which in manufacturing is the gross value of the product minus the costs of raw materials and energy. Productivity is much higher in MDC's because of higher technology and capital intensive industries. Production in LDC's is still very labor intensive.

Development requires access to raw materials although some developed countries such as Japan, Singapore and Switzerland, lack significant resources; some developing countries such as those in sub-Saharan Africa have significant raw materials. Development also requires energy to fuel industry and transform raw materials into finished products.

Countries that produce more quality nonessential consumer goods are able to promote expansion of industry and the generation of additional wealth. Consumer goods such as automobiles, telephones, and televisions are very accessible to many people in MDC's but only to the few who are wealthy in LDC's.

Education and health are key social indicators of development. High levels of development are associated with high levels of education. The quality of education is typically measured by student/teacher ratio and literacy rates. The **literacy rate** is the percentage of a country's population who can read and write. Literacy rates in MDC's usually exceed 98% whereas many LDC's have rates that are below 60%. There are also huge differences between literacy rates for men and women in developing countries. People are also healthier in more developed countries because they have better nutrition and access to health care.

The United Nations' HDI includes life expectancy as a measure of development. Other demographic indicators include infant mortality, natural increase, and crude birth rates. Life expectancy is a measure of health and welfare; some developed countries have life expectancies that are twice as high as developing countries. Infant mortality rates speak to levels of health care in a country. Rates of natural increase are much higher in LDC's and force them to allocate increasing percentages of their GDP's to care for a rapidly expanding population. Developing countries have higher rates of natural increase because they have higher crude birth rates. One has to be careful when looking at crude death rates to help measure levels of development for two reasons. Firstly the diffusion of medical technology from MDC's to LDC's has reduced death rates in less developed countries. Secondly the high crude death rates of some MDC's are a reflection of their higher percentages of elderly and lower percentages of children.

Key Issue 2 – Where are more and less developed countries distributed?

VI. Industrialization and Economic Development

B. Contemporary patterns and impacts of industrialization and development
2. Variations in levels of development

Development is the process of economic growth, where countries try to improve their level of material wealth through the diffusion and realization of resources, knowledge, and technology. It is a continuous process and each country lies somewhere along that continuum. A **more developed country** (**MDC** and also known as a **developed country**) will be further along that continuum than a **less developed country** (**LDC** and also known as a **developing country**).

The **Human Development Index (HDI)** is one measure of development. It was created by the United Nations and calculates development in terms of human welfare rather than money or productivity. It evaluates human welfare in three areas: economic, social, and demographic. The economic factor is **gross domestic product** per capita (GDP); the social factors are the **literacy rate** and amount of education; and the demographic factor is life expectancy. The highest HDI possible is 1.0 or 100% and the countries of the world can be categorized into nine regions according to their level of development.

VI. Industrialization and Economic Development

B. Contemporary patterns and impacts of industrialization and development
1. Spatial organization of the world economy
2. Variations in levels of development

Five of the nine regions identified by the United Nations HDI are more developed. These include North America, Europe, Russia, Japan, and the Oceania. North America has the highest HDI (0.95) and is well endowed with natural resources and agricultural land. It has developed high-tech industries, and is a leading consumer and the world's largest market. Its high percentage of tertiary sector employment has offset the loss of manufacturing.

During the Cold War Europe was regarded as two regions. With the fall of communism, the two parts of Europe have become much closer. Europe has a very high HDI (0.94). Europe has become the world's largest and richest market with the elimination of most economic barriers through the European Union. Levels of development are highest in western and northern Europe. Europe is dependent on international trade and, to pay for imports, it produces high-value goods and services. The recent recession has exacerbated regional and national differences. Unemployment has been particularly severe in southern and eastern Europe.

Russia struggled to transition to a market economy after the dissolution of the Soviet Union in 1991, and its HDI actually declined. It has now experienced a few years of growth and now has an HDI of 0.81. However the severe worldwide recession caused a sharp drop in demand, and its HDI could decline again.

Japan has become a great economic power despite lacking key resources. It has developed a skilled labor force that specializes in high-quality and high-value products. Japan has an HDI of 0.96. Australia and New Zealand share many cultural characteristics with Britain although their economies, which are net exporters of food and other resources, are increasingly tied to Asian countries. Oceania has an HDI of 0.86.

The six regions that can be classified as less developed include Latin America, East Asia, Central Asia, Southwest Asia and North Africa, Southeast Asia, South Asia, and sub-Saharan Africa in order of development level.

A higher percentage of people in Latin America, with an HDI of 0.81, live in urban areas than any other developing region. Development in this region is also characterized by tremendous inequality in income distribution. In East Asia which has an HDI of 0.76, China is now the world's second largest economy, and the largest market for consumer products. Manufacturing has moved to this region because of low wages which is driving down factory pay around the world. There are also regional economic equalities in China.

Most of the countries of Central Asia were once part of the Soviet Union. Levels of development in Kazakhstan and Iran are relatively high, especially because of petroleum production. In the other republics minerals and agricultural products are the main economic resources. Afghanistan probably has one of the world's lowest HDI's. The regions HDI is 0.75.

The harsh physical environment of Southwest Asia and North Africa, with an HDI of 0.67, does not support high population concentrations but the region has the largest percentage of the world's petroleum reserves. This allows many countries in the region to enjoy a trade surplus and use petroleum wealth to finance economic development. However there is a large gap in per capita income between the petroleum-rich countries and those that lack resources. These countries have to deal with traditional cultural values associated with Islam which can hinder development, especially where the role of women is concerned. The region suffers from serious internal cultural disputes. Southwest Asia has also struggled with terrorism.

Indonesia, Vietnam, and Thailand are the most populous countries in Southeast Asia (HDI of 0.72), a region that concentrates on the production of agricultural products that are used in manufacturing. Some countries in this region, including Thailand, Singapore, Malaysia, and the Philippines, have developed rapidly especially because of growing manufacturing built on cheap labor. Economic growth in the region has slowed since the last years of the twentieth century. South Asia (HDI of 0.59) has the second-highest population and the second-lowest per capita income. India is one of the world's leading rice and wheat producers thanks in large part to the innovations of the Green Revolution. It now has the world's fourth largest economy.

With an HDI of 0.47, sub-Saharan Africa is the poorest region in the world, although it is a major source of mineral wealth. Many of the region's economic and political problems are legacies of the colonial era. The tropical and dry climates of the region are not capable of supporting large concentrations of people, but sub-Saharan Africa has the highest rate of natural increase in the world.

Key Issue 3 – Where does level of development vary by gender?

VI. Industrialization and Economic Development

B. Contemporary patterns and impacts of industrialization and development
2. Variations in levels of development
8. Women in Development

The **Gender-Related Development Index (GDI)** combines the same indicators of development used in the HDI adjusted to reflect differences in the accomplishments and conditions of men and women. Thus there are economic, social, and demographic indicators of gender differences in the GDI. A country with complete gender equality would have a GDI of 1.0. A country with a high GDI means that both men and women in that country have achieved a high level of development. The lowest GDIs, where women's level of development is substantially below that of men, are in sub-Saharan Africa.

The **Gender Empowerment Measure (GEM)** measures the degree of economic and political power held by women. The GEM economic indicator is the percentage of women in professional and technical jobs. This indicator is much higher in MDCs than in LDCs. One indicator of the political power of women is the percentage of the country's administrative and managerial jobs they hold. This is higher in MDCs, especially Europe, than LDCs. The other political indicator of empowerment is the percentage of women elected to public office. Key indicators look better for LDCs now than a generation ago, but the gap in key development indicators between LDCs and MDCs remains wide.

Key Issue 4 – Why do less developed countries face obstacles to development?

VI. Industrialization and Economic Development

A. Growth and diffusion of industrialization
4. Geographic critiques of models of economic localization

B. Contemporary patterns and impacts of industrialization and development
7. Local development initiatives: government policies

For much of the 20th century self sufficiency or balanced growth was the most popular development alternative, especially for LDCs. It protects infant industries by setting barriers and tariffs on imports, as well as fixing quotas and requiring licenses to restrict the number of legal importers. India followed this model of development in the decades after independence from Britain. It has two major problems. It protects inefficient industries and creates a large bureaucracy to administer the various controls.

Development through international trade takes a very different approach. By following this approach a country can develop its unique economic assets and use the funds from these exports to finance other development.

In the 1950's W.W. Rostow proposed his **development model** which helped countries to move towards development through international trade. This was a five-stage model. Stage one was a traditional society where a country was still predominantly agricultural. In stage two a country reaches the preconditions for takeoff when entrepreneurs initiate economic activities. Infrastructure develops and productivity increases. Stage three is takeoff which is essentially the beginning of an Industrial Revolution. In the drive to maturity stage industry diffuses and results in rapid growth. According to Rostow the final stage is the age of mass consumption when the economy shifts from heavy industry to the production of consumer goods. This model was based on the belief that MDCs in Western Europe and Anglo-America would be followed by countries in Eastern Europe and Japan. Also, many LDCs have an abundance of raw materials that would generate funds to promote development in these countries.

Richard Nolan's **stages of growth model** is similar to Rostow's model. It has six stages but focuses more on increased technology as a society develops.

The international trade approach has been followed by numerous countries in Asia. The most successful initially in Asia included South Korea, Singapore, Taiwan and Hong Kong (then a British colony). They concentrated on the production of manufacturing goods using cheap labor. The petroleum-rich Arab countries pursued the same approach. Saudi Arabia, Kuwait, Bahrain, Oman, and the United Arab Emirates have been very successful, using petroleum revenues to finance large-scale projects.

The international trade approach to development also has problems. These include uneven resource distribution, market stagnation, and increased dependence on MDCs. But it has now been embraced by most countries. This approach has been aided by the creation of the **World Trade Organization (WTO)** in 1995 which helps to reduce barriers to international trade. The WTO helps to eliminate trade restrictions between countries. It also enforces international trade agreements.

Investment made by **transnational corporations (TNCs)** in foreign countries is known as **foreign direct investment (FDI)**. Of the 500 largest TNCs in 2008, 153 had headquarters in the United States in 2005 and 189 in Europe.

LDCs borrow money for major projects from two major international lenders. The **World Bank** includes the International Bank for Reconstruction and Development (IBRD) and the International Development Association (IDA). They provide loans for the reform of public administration and legal institutions. The **International Monetary Fund (IMF)** provides loans to countries that have balance-of-payment problems rather than for specific projects. There are numerous problems associated with all of these loans. Many new projects in LDCs are expensive failures, and many LDCs have been unable to repay interest and loans. Neither of these organizations will cancel or refinance debts without strings attached. Before granting debt relief, an LDC is required to prepare a Policy Framework Paper (PFP) outlining a **structural adjustment program** which includes economic goals and strategies for achieving the objectives.

Fair trade has been proposed as an alternative to the international trade model of development. **Fair trade** means that products are made and traded according to standards that protect workers and small businesses in LDCs. Standards for fair trade are set internationally by Fairtrade Labelling Organizations International (FLO). Ten Thousand Villages, which specializes in handicrafts, is the largest fair trade organization in North America. Two sets of standards distinguish fair trade; one set applies to workers on farms and in factories and the other to producers.

The world is clearly divided into regions that have differing levels of economic development. The **core-periphery model** explains this in a simplified way. The wealthiest countries are the core and the less developed countries are on the periphery. There are some countries, like Chile, Brazil, and China that don't easily fit into either and are thus sometimes described as **semi-peripheral**. Immanuel **Wallerstein's World Systems Theory** is similar to the core-periphery model. Wallerstein believed that the concept of core-periphery developed in the 15th century as Europeans began to explore and control the globe. His theory describes the world as an interdependent system of countries linked by political and economic competition. **Dependency theory** speaks to continued dependency of LDCs on MDCs where the elite in a developing country will control the vast majority of the wealth and resources of that country.

KEY TERMS

Core-periphery model
Dependency theory
Developed country
Developing country
Development
Fair trade
Foreign direct investment
Gender Empowerment Measure
(GEM)
Gender-Related Development Index
(GDI)
Gross domestic product (GDP)
Human Development Index (HDI)
International Monetary Fund (IMF)
Less developed country (LDC)

Literacy rate
More developed country (MDC)
Nolan's stages of growth model
Primary sector
Productivity
Rostow's Development Model
Secondary sector
Semi-periphery
Structural adjustment program
Tertiary sector
Transnational corporation
Value added
Wallerstein's World Systems Theory
World Bank
World Trade Organization (WTO)

Key Issues Revisited

1. Why does development vary among countries?
-development is the process by which the material conditions of a country's people are improved
-an MDC has a higher level of per capita GDP as a result of the structural transformation of the economy from an agricultural to a service-providing society
-MDCs use their wealth to provide better health, education, and welfare services whereas LDCs must use their additional wealth largely to meet the most basic needs of a rapidly growing population

2. Where are more and less developed countries distributed?
-the five regions of MDCs include Europe, North America, Japan, Oceania, and Russia
-the seven regions of LDCs are Latin America, East Asia, Central Asia, Southwest Asia, Southeast Asia, South Asia, and sub-Saharan Africa

3. Where does level of development vary by gender?
-the United Nations has found evidence of gender inequality in every country of the world
-women have lower levels of income, literacy, and education than men
-even in countries where women have achieved near-equality with men, they still have much less economic and political power

4. Why do less developed countries face obstacles to development?
-LDCs choose between the international trade and self-sufficiency paths towards development; either way they have to borrow major funds to promote development
-the inability of LDCs to pay back loans causes considerable tension between LDCs and MDCs

Chapter 10: Agriculture

This chapter deals with the major primary sector economic activity – agriculture. The origins and diffusion of agriculture are considered first. Farming varies around the world because of a variety of cultural and physical environmental factors. Agriculture is very different in less and more developed regions. In less developed regions, dominated by subsistence agriculture, farm products are usually consumed near to where they are produced. Commercial farming is the norm in more developed countries and farmers sell what they produce. Farmers face numerous problems in each type of region.

Key Issue 1 – Where did agriculture originate?

V. Agriculture and Rural Land Use

A. Development and diffusion of agriculture
1. Neolithic Agricultural Revolution

Prior to the invention of agriculture, humans lived as nomadic **hunters and gatherers**, traveling in small groups and collecting food daily. Over thousands of years, plant cultivation evolved through a combination of accident and deliberate experiment. In this way, about 10,000 years ago, people started to practice **agriculture**, the deliberate modification of the Earth's surface through the cultivation of plants and **domestication** of animals, for sedentary food production. This is known as the **Neolithic (or First) Agricultural Revolution.** The word *cultivate* means "to care for," and a **crop** is any plant cultivated by people.

According to the geographer Carl Sauer, there were two initial types of cultivation. The first was **vegetative planting**, which is the reproduction of plants by direct cloning from existing plants. **Seed agriculture** came later; this is the reproduction of plants of seeds. This is practiced by most farmers today.

There were probably a number of **agricultural hearths** for both vegetative planting and seed agriculture. Sauer believes that vegetative planting originated in South-East Asia and diffused from there to other parts of Asia, the Middle East, Africa, and Southern Europe. There may have been other independent vegetative hearths in West Africa and South America.

Sauer identified numerous hearths for seed agriculture, in Asia, Africa, and the Americas. Agriculture had multiple hearths because, to a certain extent, the physical environment determines the food that will be produced.

V. Agriculture and Rural Land Use

A. Development and diffusion of agriculture
2. Second Agricultural Revolution
4. Modern commercial agriculture

D. Modern commercial agriculture

2. Spatial organization and diffusion of industrial agriculture

In **subsistence agriculture**, found in less developed countries (LDC's), farmers produce goods to provide for themselves and others in the local community. **Commercial agriculture**, found in more developed countries (MDC's), is the production of food for competitive, free market sale. This type of agriculture emerged as a result of increased farming technology that was developed during the **Second Agricultural Revolution** in the years preceding the Industrial Revolution in 18th century Europe. In **planned agricultural economies**, which are associated with communist countries, the government controls the supply and price of agricultural goods.

Five principal features distinguish commercial from subsistence agriculture. Firstly, as mentioned above, the purpose of farming is different in LDC's and MDC's. Secondly, agriculture in LDC's is more **labor intensive** rather than the **capital intensive** agriculture which is the norm in MDC's. Thus there will always be a higher percentage of the labor force involved in agriculture in the developing world. Thirdly and related to the percentage of farmers in the labor force, agriculture in developed countries involves more machinery and technology. Fourthly, farm size is larger in commercial agriculture, especially in the United States and Canada. The loss of very productive farmland, known as **prime agricultural land**, is an increasing problem in the United States because of urban sprawl. Finally in commercial agriculture there is a close relationship between agriculture and other businesses. This is not the case in subsistence agriculture. In developed countries the system of commercial farming is called **agribusiness** because farming is integrated into a large food production industry.

Key Issue 2 – Where are agricultural regions in less developed countries?

V. Agriculture and Rural Land use

B. Major agricultural production regions
1. Agricultural systems associated with major bioclimatic zones

C. Rural land use and settlement patterns
3. Land use/land cover change, irrigation, conservation (desertification, deforestation)

Shifting cultivation is practiced in much of the world's tropical regions. Farmers clear land for planting by slashing vegetation and burning the debris; this is called **slash and burn agriculture**. The cleared land is called **swidden** and crops grown will include rice (Asia), maize and manioc (South America), millet and sorghum (Africa). Farmers will only grow crops on a cleared field for a few years until the soil nutrients are depleted and then they will leave it **fallow** (nothing planted) so that it can recover. Shifting cultivation occupies about one-fourth of the world's land area, but supports less than 5% of the world's population. As rainforests are being cut, shifting cultivation is declining, especially in the Amazon basin. It is being replaced by logging, cattle ranching, and cash crops.

Pastoral nomadism is another type of **extensive subsistence agriculture** that involves nomadic **animal husbandry**. It is practiced in the dry climates of the developing world. The livestock provide food, clothing, and shelter. The animals will vary depending on cultural preferences and physical geography but may include goats, camels, horses, sheep, or cattle. Pastoral nomads have a strong sense of territoriality which determines the land that they occupy. Some pastoral nomads practice **transhumance** which is the seasonal movement of livestock between mountains and lowland pasture areas. **Pasture** is grass or other plants grown for feeding livestock, as well as land used for grazing. This type of agricultural system is on the decline as modern technology is resulting in the conversion of land from nomadic to sedentary agriculture.

Some subsistence agriculture is **intensive** where farmers work land more intensively to subsist. **Intertillage** or field clearance, is usually very labor intensive because of a lack of modern machinery. **Intensive subsistence agriculture** is practiced in much of Asia on small plots and mostly by hand. **Wet rice** is the dominant crop in Southeast Asia including China. Wet rice is planted in dry soil in a nursery and then moved to seedlings in a flooded field. The flooded field is called a **sawah** (**paddy** is the Malay word for wet rice).When the rice is harvested the husks, known as **chaff**, are separated from the seeds when their heads are **threshed** by being beaten on the ground. When the threshed rice is placed on a tray, the lighter chaff is **winnowed** or blown away by the wind. If the rice is to be consumed by the farmer, the **hull**, or outer covering, is removed by mortar and pestle. In parts of Asia farmers can get two harvests per year from one field. This is known as **double cropping**. Where wet rice is not dominant in Asia, more than one harvest can be obtained each year through **crop rotation** which is the practice of using different fields from crop to crop each year to avoid soil exhaustion.

Plantation agriculture is the only significant large-scale commercial agriculture in the developing world. Plantations will specialize in crops that will usually be exported to other countries such as sugarcane and coffee. They have typically been owned by foreign companies and are very labor intensive.

Key Issue 3 – Where are agricultural regions in more developed countries?

V. Agriculture and Rural Land Use

A. Development and diffusion of agriculture
4. Modern commercial agriculture

B. Major agricultural production regions
1. Agricultural systems associated with major bioclimatic zones

C. Rural land use and settlement patterns
3. Land use/land cover change, irrigation, conservation (desertification, deforestation)

D. Modern commercial agriculture
2. Spatial organization and diffusion of industrial agriculture

Mixed crop and livestock farming is practiced in much of the United States and Northern Europe. Most of the crops are fed to animals. Corn (maize) is generally the crop of choice because of its high yields per area, followed by soybeans.

Dairy farming is an important type of commercial agriculture near urban areas in North America and Europe. The ring surrounding a city from which milk can be supplied without spoiling is called the **milkshed**. Increasingly in the developed world, thanks to modern transportation systems, dairy production can take place further from the market. Dairy farmers are facing economic difficulties because of declining revenues and increasing costs. Other problems inherent to dairy farming include the fact that it is very labor intensive (cows must be milked twice a day), as well as the need for expensive **winter feed**.

Commercial grain farming, which includes wheat and corn, takes place in western North America and southern Russia. In North America there is a **winter wheat** belt in Kansas, Colorado, and Oklahoma where the crop is planted in the autumn. In the **spring wheat** belt, which includes the Dakotas, Montana, and southern Saskatchewan, the crop is planted in the spring. A third important grain growing region is in the state of Washington. Large-scale wheat production was first made possible by the McCormick **reaper** in the 1830's. Today the **combine** performs the three tasks of reaping, threshing, and cleaning in one operation.

Livestock ranching is the extensive commercial grazing of livestock land in semiarid or arid lands. It is practiced in much of the western United States and the pampas regions of Argentina, southern Brazil, and Uruguay. Historically ranching involved the herding of cattle over open ranges in a semi-nomadic style, and later became sedentary farming by dividing open land into ranches. Today it has become part of the meat-processing industry rather than an economic activity practiced on isolated farms. **Feedlots** are often used for more cost efficient livestock fattening.

Mediterranean agriculture, practiced in the Mediterranean, California, and parts of Chile, Australia, and South Africa, consists of diverse specialty crops such as grapes, olives, nuts, fruits, and vegetables mostly for human consumption. **Horticulture** is the term for the growing of fruits, vegetables, and flowers.

Commercial gardening and fruit farming is the dominant form of agriculture in the Southeastern United States. It is practiced close to urban areas and is also called **truck farming** because "truck" was the Middle English word for barter or the exchange of commodities. Truck farms grow fruits and vegetables.

Key Issue 4 – Why do farmer face economic difficulties?

V. Agricultural and Rural Land Use

C. Rural land use and settlement patterns
1. Models of agricultural land use, including von Thunen's model

The **von Thunen model** helps to explain the importance of proximity to market and the choice of crops in commercial agriculture. Johann von Thunen published his model in a book titled *The Isolated State* in 1826. According to von Thunen, rent, or land value, will decrease the further one gets from a market. Thus the agricultural products that use the land most intensively, have the highest transportation costs, are more perishable, and are in the greatest demand, such as dairying and fruits and vegetables, will be located close to the market. Agriculture that uses the land more extensively, such as livestock ranching, will be further away from the market.

Von Thunen placed horticulture and dairying closest to the city, followed by forestry (for fuel and building). The next rings were used for various crops and pasture becoming more extensive further from the market. The model had various assumptions that may not have been true in reality, such as a uniform landscape, equal ease of transportation in all directions, and a single market.

Although *The Isolated State* is a dated and oversimplified model of reality, the principles of agricultural location still apply today especially at a national or global scale, and it still describes the actual patterns of land use surrounding many cities.

V. Agriculture and Rural Land Use

B. Major agricultural production regions
2. Variations within major zones and effects of markets

D. Modern commercial agriculture
1. Biotechnology, including genetically modified plants and animals
3. Organic farming and local food production

Agricultural regions are largely determined by climate and, to a lesser extent cultural preferences. In addition there are two important economic considerations for subsistence farmers. These include rapid population growth and the demands of the international market.

According to Esther Boserup as population has increased in subsistence economies, farmers have intensified production by leaving land fallow for shorter periods and by the adoption of new farming methods.

In some LDCs such as Kenya, families may divide by gender between traditional subsistence agriculture and the growing of crops for export. Women practice most of the subsistence agriculture while men grow crops for export, one of the legacies of colonial agricultural systems, or work in urban jobs. The export crops grown in some LDCs, especially in Latin America and Asia, are those that can be converted to drugs.

Sub-Saharan African countries have been encouraged by the United States to increase their food supply in part by increased use of **biotechnology** or **genetic modification (GM)** of crops and livestock which could increase yields, nutrition, and provide more resistance to pests.

Overproduction is a problem in commercial farming, especially the United States and Europe. Even though demand has remained constant, the U.S. government has tried to alleviate the problem by developing three policies. Farmers are encouraged to avoid producing crops that are in excess supply. The government will pay farmers when certain prices are low, and they will buy surplus production and sell or donate it to foreign governments.

   Sustainable agriculture is becoming more widespread in MDCs. This type of agriculture promotes environmental quality through sensitive land management, limited use of chemicals, and integrating the growing of crops and raising of livestock. One type of land management is **ridge tillage** which is the planting of crops on ridge tops to conserve soil.

V. Agriculture and Rural Land Use

A. Development and diffusion of agriculture
3. Green Revolution

B. Major agricultural production regions
3. Linkages and flows among regions of food production and consumption.

C. Rural land use and settlement patterns
3. Land use/land cover change, irrigation, conservation (desertification, deforestation)

D. Modern commercial agriculture
2. Spatial organization and diffusion of industrial agriculture
4. Environmental impacts of agriculture

   Food supply can be increased in the world by initiating a number of strategies. Expansion of land under production is one method, although this can lead to environmental problems such as **desertification** in arid regions. Soil salinity has also been a problem where irrigated agriculture is practiced in hot, arid regions. The **Green Revolution** (also known as the **Third Agricultural Revolution**) which involved the use of new higher-yield seeds as well as fertilizers during the 1970's and 1980's has resulted in increased food supply in parts of Asia and Latin America. Strategies are now being developed to expand **aquaculture,** fish farming or the cultivation of the oceans. Higher-protein cereals are being developed in MDCs, and the palatability of rarely consumed foods, like soybean, is being improved. Another alternative for increasing the world's food supply is to export more food from MDCs that produce surpluses to LDCs, especially in Africa that are experiencing a food-supply crisis.

KEY TERMS

Agribusiness

Agriculture

Agricultural hearths

Animal husbandry

Aquaculture

Biotechnology

Capital-intensive

Cereal grain

Chaff

Combine

Commercial agriculture

Commercial gardening and fruit farming

Commercial grain farming

Crop

Crop rotation

Dairy farming

Desertification

Domestication

Double cropping

Extensive subsistence agriculture

Fallow

Feedlots

Genetic modification (GM)

Grain

Green Revolution

Horticulture

Hull

Hunters and gatherers

Intensive subsistence agriculture

Intertillage

Labor-intensive

Livestock ranching

Mediterranean agriculture

Milkshed

Mixed crop and livestock farming

Neolithic Agricultural Revolution

Paddy

Pastoral nomadism

Pasture

Planned agricultural economies

Plantation

Prime agricultural land

Ranching

Reaper

Ridge tiller

Sawah

Second Agricultural Revolution

Seed agriculture

Slash-and-burn agriculture

Shifting cultivation

Spring wheat

Subsistence agriculture

Sustainable agriculture

Swidden

Third Agricultural Revolution

Thresh

Transhumance

Truck farming

Vegetative planting

Von Thunen Model

Wet rice

Winnow

Winter feed

Winter wheat

Key Issues Revisited

1. Where did agriculture originate?
-before the development of agriculture, people survived by hunting and gathering
-agriculture resulted from thousands of years of experiments and accidents
-current agricultural practices vary between MDCs and LDCs

2. Where are agricultural regions in LDCs?
-most people in LDCs are subsistence farmers, growing crops primarily to feed themselves
-important types of subsistence agriculture include shifting cultivation, pastoral nomadism, and intensive farming
-regions where subsistence agriculture is practiced are characterized by a large percentage of the labor force engaged in agriculture

3. Where are agricultural regions in MDCs?
-the most common type of farm found in MDCs is mixed crop and livestock
-where mixed crop and livestock is not suitable, commercial farmers practice a variety of other types of agriculture, including dairying, commercial grain, and ranching

4. Why do farmers face economic difficulties?
-problems with agriculture in LDCs are associated with rapid population growth and pressure to adopt international trade strategies to promote development
-problems with agriculture in MDCs result from access to markets and overproduction

Chapter 11: Industry

This chapter outlines the regions where industry is located and why. The two most important considerations regarding location are where the markets for the products are located and where the necessary resources are located. Increasingly industry has diffused from MDCs to LDCs, especially through the operation of transnational corporations.

Key Issue 1 – Where is industry distributed?

VI. Industrialization and Economic Development

A. Growth and diffusion of industrialization
2. Industrial Revolution

The **Industrial Revolution** originated in Britain during the late 18th century because of the combination of entrepreneurs, capital, raw materials, and available labor. It also included social and political changes but it generally refers to the economic changes that began in Britain in the late 1700's. Prior to the Industrial Revolution small-scale manufacturing was home-based and known as the **cottage industry**. The Industrial Revolution resulted in major changes for the iron and steel industry, coal mining, transportation, textiles, chemicals, and food processing.

VI. Industrialization and Economic Development

A. Growth and diffusion of industrialization
1. The changing role of energy and technology
3. Evolution of economic cores and peripheries

B. Contemporary patterns and impacts of industrialization and development
1. Spatial organization of the world economy

Each of the following three regions accounts for roughly one-fourth of the world's total industrial output: Europe, North America, and East Asia.

Western Europe has major industrialization regions in Britain, the Rhine-Ruhr Valley, the mid-Rhine, and northern Italy. Britain's is the oldest of these industrial regions, and with the decline of traditional industry it was able to attract high-tech industries in the late twentieth century, especially Japanese companies. The Rhine-Ruhr has been important largely because of coal and iron deposits, and steel making. The mid-Rhine includes parts of Germany and France, and has been important because of its proximity to large consumer markets. The Po valley of northern Italy began with **textile** manufacturing and has benefited from low labor costs. Northeastern Spain was Western Europe's fastest growing industrial area in the late twentieth century, especially in the motor-vehicle industry.

The oldest industrial areas in Eastern Europe are the Central industrial district which is centered on Moscow, and the St. Petersburg industrial district which was one of Russia's early nodes of industrial development. Other industrial areas in Eastern Europe include the Volga industrial district, particularly important for petroleum and natural gas, and the Ural industrial district, which has become a main source of raw materials but lacks energy sources. The Kuznetsk is Russia's most important industrial region east of the Ural Mountains. Outside the former Soviet Union there are important industrial regions in Donetsk, Eastern Ukraine, and Silesia which includes parts of Poland and the Czech Republic.

North America became a major industrial region later than Europe. Textiles were important in the United States by 1860. Manufacturing has been traditionally located in the northeastern United States with its numerous raw materials. These areas include New England, the Middle Atlantic, the Mohawk Valley, and the Pittsburgh-Lake Erie region. The Western Great Lakes have also become important, especially because of the dominance of Chicago as a market center. Southern California is the leading U.S. industrial area outside of the Northeast. Canada's most important industrial area is in Southeastern Ontario, benefiting from its location and the availability of cheap hydroelectric power.

East Asia has become a major industrial region since the second half of the 20th century by taking advantage of its large labor force. Japan emerged first, followed by South Korea, Taiwan, and China. The latter is now the world's largest manufacturer of textiles and apparel, steel, and many household products. It also has the world's largest supply of low-cost labor and the world's largest market for many consumer products.

Key Issue 2 – Why are situation factors important?

VI. Industrialization and Economic Development

A. Growth and diffusion of industrialization
4. Geographic critiques of models of economic localization

B. Contemporary patterns and impacts of industrialization and development
1. Spatial organization of the world economy

Situation factors involve decisions about industrial location that attempt to minimize transportation costs by considering raw material source(s) as well as the market(s). If the cost of transporting the inputs is greater than the cost of transporting the finished product, the best plant location is nearer to the inputs. Otherwise the best location for the factory will be closer to the consumers.

The North American copper industry is a good example of locating near the raw material source. Copper concentration is a **bulk-reducing industry**; the final product weighs less than the inputs. Two-thirds of U.S. copper is mined in Arizona so most of the concentration mills and smelters are also in Arizona. Steelmaking is another bulk-reducing industry. Steel was made by the Bessemer process, invented in 1855, which combined iron ore and carbon at very high temperatures using coal to produce steel. By the beginning of the 20th century most large U.S. steel mills were located near the East and West coasts because iron ore was coming from other countries.

Today the U.S steel industry is located near major markets in minimills. It has become a **footloose industry**, which can locate virtually anywhere because the main input is scrap metal and is available almost everywhere. Today the U.S. steel industry takes advantage of **agglomeration economies**, or sharing of services with other companies that are available at major markets. The agglomeration of companies can lead to the development of **ancillary activities** that surround and support large-scale industry. This will result in continued growth which is called **cumulative causation**. **Deglomeration** occurs when a firm leaves an agglomerated region to start in a distant, new place. However, according to Alfred Weber's theory of industrial location or **least-cost theory**, firms will locate where they can minimize transportation and labor costs as well as take advantage of agglomeration economies.

The location of **bulk-gaining industries** is determined largely by the markets because they gain volume or weight during production. Most drink bottling industries are examples of bulk-gaining industries; empty cans or bottles are brought to the bottler, filled and shipped to consumers.

Single-market manufacturers are specialized, with only one or two customers, such as manufacturers of motor vehicle parts. Obviously they will tend to cluster around their customers. Perishable-product industries such as fresh food and newspapers will usually locate near their markets.

Transportation costs will decline with distance because loading and unloading costs are the greatest. The major modes of transportation are ship, rail, truck, and air. A **break-of-bulk point** is a place transfer from one mode of transportation to another is possible.

Key Issue 3 – Why are site factors important?

VI. Industrialization and Economic Development

A. Growth and diffusion of industrialization
1. The changing roles of energy and technology

B. Contemporary patterns and impacts of industrialization and development
1. Spatial organization of the world economy
5. Natural resources and environmental concerns

Site factors include labor, land, and capital. **Labor-intensive industries** are those where the highest percentage of expenses are the cost of employees, such as textile and apparel production. Land, which includes natural resources, is a major site factor. City sites offer proximity to a large supply of labor as well as to sources of capital. More recently factories are locating in suburban and rural locations because land is cheaper and proximity to highways is more important now. There are also important environmental factors. For example, aluminum producers locate near dams to take advantage of hydroelectric power. The availability of capital is critical to the location of high-tech industries such as those in California's Silicon Valley. The distribution of industries in LDCs is largely dependent on the ability to borrow money.

Key Issue 4 – Why are location factors changing?

VI. Industrialization and Economic Development

A. Growth and diffusion of industrialization
1. The changing roles of energy and technology

B. Contemporary patterns and impacts of industrialization and development
1. Spatial organization of the world economy
3. Deindustrialization and economic restructuring
4. Globalization and international division of labor

      Within regions in MDCs industry has relocated to urban peripheries and rural areas from central city locations. At the interregional level manufacturing has moved towards the south and west in the United States. Historically industrial growth has been encouraged in the South by government policies to reduce regional disparities. Southern states have enacted **right-to-work laws** that require factories to maintain an "open shop" and prohibit a "closed shop." In a closed shop everyone who works in the factory has to join the union. Thus Southern right-to-work laws have made it much more difficult for unions to organize, collect dues, and bargain. States that have passed these laws are called **right-to-work states**.

      In Western Europe government policies and those of the European Union have also encouraged industry to move from traditional industrial centers in northwestern Europe toward southern and eastern Europe. For example Spain's textile and motor-vehicle manufacturing industries have grown substantially since its admission to the European Union in 1986. Some Central European countries such as Poland, the Czech Republic, and Hungary, have received industrial investment since the fall of communism in the early 1990's. They offer less skilled but cheaper labor than Western Europe and have locations that are close to major markets.

      In 1970 nearly one-half of world industry was in Europe and nearly one-third was in North America; now these two regions account for only one-fourth each. The share of world industry in other regions has increased from one-sixth in 1970 to one-half in 2010. These regions include East Asia, South Asia, and Latin America.

      As industry has declined in MDCs, it has increased in LDCs. In 1980 80% of the world's steel was produced in MDCs. Between 1980 and 2008, MDCs share of steel production declined to 40%, and that of LDCs increased to 60%.

      China is the leading new industrial center in the world because of its low labor costs and vast consumer market. Mexico and Brazil are the leading industrial centers in Latin America, with manufacturing clustered near large cities such as Mexico City and Sao Paulo. Since the 1980's manufacturing in Mexico has moved north to take advantage of the U.S. market, and **maquiladora** plants have been established close to the U.S. border. Maquiladoras, which assemble U.S. parts and ship the finished product back to the United States, have benefited from the **North American Free Trade Agreement (NAFTA)**. NAFTA has eliminated restrictions on the flow of materials and products between the United States and Mexico.

The cost of labor is changing the spatial organization of industry around the world. This is particularly true of the textile and apparel industry. In the 20th century production in the United States moved from the Northeast to the Southeast to take advantage of cheaper wages. More recently the apparel industry is located in Latin America, China, and other Asian countries. Now the United States imports more than 75% of its clothing needs. This is one part of the **new international division of labor**. Industrial jobs are transferring to LDCs largely as a result of transnational corporations' search for low-cost labor. **Transnational corporations** are **outsourcing**, turning over much of the responsibility for production to independent suppliers. There is concern that some of these clothes are made in factories called **sweatshops**, not unlike those in the early Industrial Revolution, where the working conditions are terrible.

In some MDCs industry is remaining in traditional regions because of skilled labor and rapid delivery to market. The **Fordist** approach, named for Henry Ford, traditionally assigned each worker a specific task in mass production industry. **Post-Fordist** production has recently become the norm in MDCs. It is flexible production with skilled workers characterized by teams working together, problem solving through consensus, and factory workers being treated alike regardless of their level.

Just-in-time delivery is the shipment of parts and materials to a factory immediately before they are needs. It avoids the stocking of unnecessary and expensive inventory. Two kinds of disruption can result from reliance on just-in-time delivery: labor unrest and "Acts of God" (such as a blizzard or flood).

KEY TERMS

Agglomeration economies
Ancillary activities
Break-of-bulk point
Bulk-gaining industry
Bulk-reducing industry
Cottage industry
Cumulative causation
Deglomeration
Footloose industry
Fordist
Industrial Revolution
Just-in-time delivery
Labor-intensive industry
Least-cost theory

Maquiladora
New international division of labor
North American Free Trade Agreement (NAFTA)
Outsourcing
Post-Fordist
Right-to-work laws
Right-to-work states
Site factors
Situation factors
Sweatshops
Textile
Transnational corporations

Key Issues Revisited

1. Where is industry distributed?
-industry has been concentrated in three regions during the twentieth century –
Europe, North America, and East Asia

2. Why are situation factors important?
-factories try to identify a location where location costs are minimized
-critical industrial location costs include situation factors for some firms and site factors
for others
-situation factors involve the cost of transporting both inputs into the factory and products
from the factory to the consumer

3. Why are site factors important?
-three site factors – land, labor, and capital – control the cost of doing business at a
location

4. Why are location factors changing?
-new industrial regions are able to attract some industries, especially because of low wage
rates
-traditional industrial regions have been able to offer manufacturers skilled workers and
proximity to customers demanding just-in-time delivery

Chapter 12: Services

In MDCs most workers are employed in the tertiary sector of the economy, which is the provision of goods and services. There is a close relationship between services and settlements; most services are clustered in settlements. They are also clustered in MDCs because that is where people are more likely to be able to buy services, rather than LDCs. Within MDCs business services locate in large settlements which are also the key markets.

Key Issue 1 – Where did services originate?

VII. Cities and Urban Land Use

C. Models of internal city structure
4. Changing employment mix

In North America, three-quarters of employees work in the service sector. There are three types of services: consumer services, business services, and public services.

Consumer services provide services to individual consumers and include retail services and personal services. Retail and wholesale services include about 15% of all jobs in the United States and provide goods for sale to consumers. Other consumer services include education services, health services, and leisure and hospitality services.

Business services help other businesses and include financial services, professional services, transportation and information services; they diffuse and distribute services.

Public services which include governmental services at various levels provide security and protection for citizens and businesses.

All the growth in employment in the United States between 1972 and 2009 has been in the service sector, as employment in primary and secondary sector activities has declined. Within business services, jobs expanded most rapidly in professional services. The most rapid increase within consumer services has been in the provision of health care. There have been other large increases in education, entertainment, and recreation.

Settlements probably originated to provide consumer and public services. Business services came later.

VII. Cities and Urban Land Use
A. Development and character of cities
1. Origin of cities

There have been major urban settlements in different parts of the world since ancient times, including Mesopotamia, Greece, and Rome. In ancient Greece **city-states** such as Athens and Sparta, emerged. These included the city and surrounding countryside or hinterland. Athens made major contributions to the development of culture, philosophy, and other elements of Western civilization. This shows that urban settlements have been distinguished from rural ones not only by public services but also by a concentration of consumer services, especially cultural activities. Cities in the Roman world, especially Rome, were important centers of administration, trade, culture, and a host of other services. Urbanization declined with the fall of Rome and didn't reemerge until the 11th century. From the time of the fall of Rome until the Industrial Revolution the largest cities in the world were in Asia.

Key Issue 2 – Where are contemporary services located?

V. Agriculture and Rural Land Use

C. Rural land use and settlement patterns
2. Settlement patterns associated with major agricultural types

A large percentage of the world's population still practice agriculture and live in rural settlements. In **clustered rural settlements**, families live to close to one another and fields surround houses and farm buildings. In **dispersed rural settlements**, farmers live on individual farms and are more isolated from their neighbors.

Circular rural settlements consist of a central open space surrounded by buildings. The medieval German *Gewandorf* settlements and East African Masai villages are examples of circular settlements. Linear rural settlements are clustered along transportation like roads or rivers. In North America most linear settlements can be traced to the original French *longlot* or *seigneurial* pattern.

Dispersed rural settlements are associated with more recent agricultural settlements in the developed world. In some European countries clustered patterns were converted to dispersed settlements. The rural **enclosure movement** that accompanied the Industrial Revolution in Britain is a good example of this transition. It provided greater efficiency in an agricultural world that relied on fewer farmers.

VII. Cities and Urban Land Use

A. Development and character of cities
1. Origin of cities
2. Rural-urban migration and urban growth
3. Global cities and megacities

C. Models of internal city structure
4. Changing employment mix
5. Changing demographic and social structures

The population of urban settlements exceeded that of rural settlements for the first time in human history in 2008. In the 1930's Louis Wirth observed major differences between urban and rural residents. He defined a **city** as a permanent settlement that has three characteristics – large size, high population, and socially heterogeneous people. In the urban world most relationships are contractual and employment is more highly specialized than in rural settlements. In MDCs social distinctions between urban and rural

96

residents has become more blurred than in LDCs because nearly everyone in an MDC is now urban.

     Urbanization is the process by which the population of cities grows, both in *numbers* and *percentage*. Today in MDCs, about three-fourths of the people live in urban areas, compared to about two-fifths in LDCs, although urbanization in Latin America is comparable to MDCs. In MDCs the process of urbanization that began around 1800 has largely ended, because the percentage living in urban areas cannot increase much more. The percentage living in cities in LDCs in recent years has increased because of rural to urban migration. Eight of the ten most populous cities in the world are currently in LDCs.

Key Issue 3 – Why are consumer services distributed in a regular pattern?

VII. Cities and Urban Land Use

B. Models of urban systems
2. Central place theory

     Consumer services are generally provided in a regular pattern based on size of settlements, with larger settlements offering more than smaller ones.

     Central place theory provides a framework for looking at the relationship between settlements of different sizes, especially their ability to provide various goods and services. It was developed by Walter Christaller in the 1930's, and was based on his studies of settlement patterns in southern Germany. A service will have a **market area** or **hinterland** of potential customers. Each urban settlement will have a market area, assuming that people will get services from the nearest settlement. The **range** is the maximum distance that people are willing to travel for a service, and the **threshold** is the minimum number of people needed to support a service. Retailers and other service providers will use these concepts to analyze the potential market-area. Determining the profitability of a location and optimal location within a market is called **market-area analysis.** Services and settlements are hierarchical, and larger settlements will provide consumer services that have larger thresholds, ranges, and market areas than smaller settlements. Central place theory shows market areas in MDCs as a series of hexagons of various sizes. Christaller identifies four different levels of market area and seven different settlement sizes. Since this is a theory he made certain assumptions that may or may not be true in reality, such as equal ease of transportation in all directions, and that people would always get a service from the nearest available market.

VII. Cities and Urban Land Use

B. Models of urban systems
3. Gravity model

     The **gravity model** predicts that the best location for a service is directly related to the number of people in the area and inversely related to the distance that people must travel for it. A place with more people will have more potential customers, and people who are further away from a service are less likely to use it.

VII. Cities and Urban Land Use

B. Models of urban systems
1. Rank-size rule

Geographers have observed that, in many MDCs, there is sometimes a regular hierarchy of settlements from largest to smallest. This is the **rank size rule**, where a country's nth-largest settlement is $1/n$th the population of the largest settlement. So the second largest city would be half the size of the largest. The hierarchy of towns and cities in the United States follows the rank size rule fairly well, which shows that goods and services are provided to consumers at many levels throughout the country. Many LDCs as well as some European countries follow the **primate city rule** rather than the rank size rule. A **primate city** is much larger and more important than any other city in that country. This is true of Buenos Aires, Argentina and Copenhagen, Denmark.

In settlements at the lower end of the central place hierarchy, **periodic markets** may be set up. These are collections of individual vendors who offer goods and services in a specific location one of two times a week. They exist all over the globe.

Key Issue 4 – Why do business services cluster in large settlements?

VII. Cities and Urban Land Use

A. Development and character of cities
3. Global cities and megacities

Modern world cities offer business services especially financial services. They also have retail services with huge market areas, such as leisure and cultural services of national importance. London presents more plays than the rest of Britain combined. World cities are also centers of national and international power. New York is the headquarters of the United Nations, and Brussels is one of the headquarter cities of the European Union.

Four levels of cities have been identified by geographers. These are world cities, command and control centers, specialized producer-service centers, and dependent centers. London, New York, and Tokyo are at the top of the hierarchy of world cities. They are dominant world cities and are unique in that they all have important international stock exchanges. There are also second and third tier world cities. Some major corporations and banks have their headquarters in second tier or major world cities. Third tier world cities are called secondary world cities.

C. Models of urban systems
4. Changing employment mix

Command and control centers contain the headquarters of large corporations, and concentrations of a variety of business services. There are regional centers like Atlanta and Boston, and subregional centers such as Charlotte and Des Moines.

Specialized producer-service centers have management, and research and development activities associated with specific industries. Detroit is a specialized producer-service center specializing in motor vehicles.

As the term suggests, dependent centers depend on decisions made in world cities for their economic wellbeing. They provide relatively unskilled jobs. San Diego is an industrial and military dependent center.

In the global economy, LDCs specialize in two distinctive types of business services - **offshore financial services** and **back-office functions**. Small countries, often islands and microstates, offer offshore financial services. These offshore centers provide tax havens for companies and privacy from disclosure. Back-office functions include processing insurance claims, payroll management, transcription work, and other routine clerical work. Some LDCs have attracted back offices because of low wages and the ability to speak English.

Basic industries are exported mainly to consumers outside a settlement and constitute that community's **economic base**. These industries employ a large percentage of a community's workforce. **Nonbasic industries** are usually consumed within that community. The growth of a community's economy that results from its basic and nonbasic industries is called the **multiplier effect**. Basic industries are vital to the economic health of a settlement. The concept of basic industries originally referred to the secondary sector of the economy, such as manufacturing but in a **postindustrial society** such as the United States, they are now more likely to be in the service sector of the economy.

KEY TERMS

Back offices	Market-area analysis
Basic industries	Multiplier effect
Business services	Nonbasic industries
Central business district (CBD)	Offshore financial services
Central place theory	Periodic markets
City	Postindustrial society
City-state	Primate city
Clustered rural settlement	Primate city rule
Consumer services	Public services
Dispersed rural settlement	Range
Economic base	Service
Enclosure movement	Settlement
Gravity model	Threshold
Hinterland	Urbanization

Key Issues Revisited

1. Where did services originate?
-consumer (including retail, health, education, and leisure), business (including financial, professional, and management), and public (including federal, state, and local) are the three types of services
-services originated in rural settlements, and the earliest services were primarily personal and public

2. Where are contemporary services located?
-services are clustered in settlements
-rural centers are centers for agriculture and provide a small number of services
-urbanization involves increases in the percentage of and the number of people living in urban settlements
-urban settlements are centers for consumer and business services

3. Why are consumer services distributed in a regular pattern?
-consumer services attract customers from market areas of varying size
-geographers calculate whether a service can be profitable within a market area
-in MDCs, market areas form a relatively regular hierarchy by size and distance from each other

4. Who do business services locate in large settlements?
-financial, professional, and other business services cluster disproportionately in large world cities to support the operations of major corporations
-world cities also play major consumer and public service functions

Chapter 13: Urban Patterns

Urban geographers are concerned with the global distribution of urban settlements as well as the distribution of people and activities within urban areas. This chapter begins by addressing why services cluster downtown. The chapter then examines models that have been developed to help explain the internal structure of urban areas in the North America and elsewhere. The distinctive problems of inner cities and suburbs are also considered.

Key Issue 1 – Why do services cluster downtown?

VII. Cities and Urban Land Use

C. Models of internal city structure
4. Changing employment mix
5. Changing demographic and social structures

The **central business district (CBD)** is the center of a city where services have traditionally clustered. Specifically three types of retail services have concentrated in the center because they require accessibility. These include services with a high threshold, those with a long range, and those that serve people who work in the center. A large department store is a service with a high threshold. Retail services with a high range are specialized shops that are patronized infrequently. Both of these types of services have moved in large numbers to suburban locations in recent years. Retailers survive in some CBDs if they combine retailing with recreational activities. This has become a reality in Boston, Baltimore, Philadelphia, and San Francisco. Services that cater to people working in the CBD have remained in this location and have actually expanded, especially where CBDs have been revitalized. Business services such as advertising and banking have also remained clustered in the CBD.

VII. Cities and Urban Land Use

C. Models of internal city structure
4. Changing employment mix
5. Changing demographic and social structures

D. Built environment and social space
1. Housing
2. Transportation and infrastructure
4. Urban planning and design

Land costs in the CBD are very high because of competition for accessibility. Thus land use is more intensive in the CBD, and some activities are excluded from the center because of the high cost of space. The built character is more vertical than other parts of urban areas, both above and below ground. Infrastructure, including transportation and utilities, typically run underground. Skyscrapers give the central city its distinctive image. Washington, D.C. is the only large U.S. CBD that does not have skyscrapers because no building is allowed to be higher than the U.S. Capitol dome. High rents and land shortages have excluded industrial and residential activities from the CBDs of North American cities. Industries that have not closed have moved their operations to the suburbs where they can take advantage of cheaper land. Residents have also moved away from CBDs. Pull factors have lured them to the suburbs; the crime and poverty of central cities have acted as a push factor. In the twenty-first century, the population of many U.S. CBDs has increased, largely as a result of urban renewal. "Empty nesters" and young professionals are particularly attracted to downtown living.

European CBDs are visibly very different because they have tried to preserve their historic cores by limiting high-rise buildings. More people live downtown outside North America, but renovation is more expensive and does not always produce enough space to meet the demand. As a result, rents are much higher in the center of European cities than in U.S. cities.

Key Issue 2 – Where are people distributed within urban areas?

VII. Cities and Urban Land Use

C. Models of internal city structure
1. Concentric zone model
2. Sector model
3. Multiple-nuclei model
5. Changing demographic and social structures

Three different models were developed in Chicago to help explain the internal spatial organization of the urban environment. The **concentric zone model** was developed in 1923 by Burgess and applies to cities that have concentric rings of development emanating outward from a core or **central business district (CBD)**. The ring immediately outside the CBD is a **zone of transition**, containing industry and poorer-quality housing. The rings each contain different kinds of urban land use and residences become more high class further away from the CBD. The underlying sociological concepts of invasion and succession help to explain how people move away from the city center as they become wealthier and are prepared to commute further.

The **sector model** was developed in 1939 by Hoyt who saw the city developing as a series of sectors rather than rings. He believed that certain areas of the city might be more attractive for various activities because of environmental factors. The sectors often followed transportation lines. Hoyt and Burgess both claimed that social patterns in Chicago supported their model.

The **multiple nuclei model** was developed by Harris and Ullman in 1945. They believed that cities lack one central core, and instead have numerous **nodes** of business and cultural activities. Although dated, these models help geographers to understand where different people live in an urban area and why they live there. Cities in MDCs as well as LDC's exhibit characteristics of these models, but no one city matches any model perfectly.

In order to apply these models to reality, accurate data needs to be available. In the United States that information is available from the U.S. Census Bureau which has divided urban areas into **census tracts** that are essentially urban neighborhoods. They provide information about the characteristics of residents living in each tract. Social scientists can compare the distributions of characteristics and create an overall picture of where different people live. This kind of study is known as **social area analysis**.

These three models were developed to describe the spatial distribution of social classes in the urban United States. However they can also be applied to urbanization outside North America. In European cities wealthier people tend to live closer to the CBD, and there is more suburban poverty. European cities are also much older and still retain their medieval city center. In LDCs the poor are also accommodated in the suburbs, whereas the wealthier live near the center of cities. European colonial policies left a heavy mark on the development of cities in LDCs.

Islamic cities, such as Mecca, were laid out surrounding a religious core. They have mosques and a bazaar or marketplace at their center with walls guarding the perimeter. In the outer rings there were secular businesses and quarters laid out for Jews, Christians, and foreigners. Some features of these cities were adaptations to the hot and dry physical environment.

In Asia, Africa, and Latin America cities combine elements of native culture, colonial rule, religion, industry, and poverty. Griffin and Ford developed a model of a **Latin American city** which shows the wealthy living close to the CBD. Industrial sectors radiate out from the CBD, and the poorest live on the urban fringe in **squatter settlements**. The latter are known by a variety of names such as *barrios*, *barriadas*, and *favelas* in Latin America, *bidonvilles* in North Africa, and *bustees* in India.

Key Issue 3 – Why do inner cities face distinctive challenges?

VII. Cities and Urban Land Use

C. Models of internal city structure
4. Changing employment mix
5. Changing demographic and social structures
6. Uneven development, ghettoization, and gentrification

D. Built environment and social space
1. Housing
2. Transportation and infrastructure
3. Political organization of urban areas
4. Urban planning and design
5. Patterns of race, ethnicity, gender, and socioeconomic status

Inner cities in the United States have a multitude of physical, social, and economic problems. One of the major physical problems is **filtering**, which is when houses are subdivided and occupied by successive waves of lower-income people. It can lead to total abandonment. As a result of filtering inner-city neighborhoods have rapidly declining populations. **Redlining** is when banks draw lines on a map to identify areas where they will refuse to loan money although the Community Reinvestment Act has essentially made this illegal.

Governments at various levels have put together grants to help the revitalization of inner-city neighborhoods. This process is called **urban renewal**. Substandard inner-city housing has been demolished and replaced with **public housing** for low-income people. Many of the public high-rise projects built during the 1950's and 1960's have since been demolished because they were considered unsafe. More recently the trend has been to renovate deteriorating inner-city houses so that they will appeal to middle-class people. This process is known as **gentrification**.

There are numerous inner-city social problems too. Many of the residents are considered an **underclass** because they are trapped in a cycle of economic and social problems. Many lack the necessary job skills for even the most basic jobs, and there are more than 3 million homeless in the United States today. This culture of poverty leads to various crimes including drug use, gangs, and other criminal activities.

Most inner-city residents cannot pay the taxes that are necessary to provide public services. A city has two choices to close the gap between the cost of services and the funding available from taxes. It can reduce services and/or raise tax revenues. Federal government contributions have helped, but these have declined substantially since the 1980's. The percentage of the budgets of the 50 largest U.S. cities supplied by the federal government declined to 6 percent in 1990 and 2000. Some state governments have increased financial assistance to cities.

A major cause of the recession that began in 2008 was the collapse in the housing market, primarily in the inner city. Compounding the problem, housing prices have fallen in the U.S. and other MDCs since their peak in 2006.

Key Issue 4 – Why do suburbs face distinctive challenges?

VII. Cities and Urban Land Use

D. Built environment and social space
3. Political organization of urban areas

Annexation is the process of legally adding land area to a city. In the U.S. most surrounding suburban lands have their own jurisdictions and want to remain legally independent of the central city. Instead of annexing peripheral areas, cities are now surrounded by suburbs. As a result, several definitions have been created to characterize cities and their suburbs. In the 1930's Louis Wirth, an urban geography, defined a **city** as a permanent settlement that has a large size, high population density, and socially heterogeneous people. Urban settlements today can be physically defined by legal boundary, as continuously built-up area, and as a functional area. Virtually all countries have a political system that recognizes cities as legal entities with fixed boundaries. In the

United States a city that is surrounded by suburbs is sometimes called a **central city**. The central city and surrounding suburbs are together called an **urbanized area**.

The U.S. Census Bureau defines the functional areas of cities for political and economic purposes. A **Metropolitan Statistical Area (MSA)** includes an urbanized area with a population of at least 50,000 with high density adjacent counties where the majority of inhabitants work in non agricultural jobs. The census has also designated smaller urban areas as **micropolitan statistical areas**. These include an urbanized area of between 10,000 and 50,000 inhabitants and adjacent counties tied to the city. A **Consolidated Metropolitan Statistical Area (CMSA)** consists of two adjacent MSAs with overlapping commuter patterns such as the Washington-Baltimore CMSA. Within a CMSA, an MSA that exceeds one million people may be classified as a **Primary Metropolitan Statistical Area (PMSA)**. The metropolitan areas of the northeastern United States now form one continuous urban complex or **megalopolis** (from the Greek word meaning great city).

Many urban regional problems cannot be easily solved because of the fragmentation of local government. There are 1,400 local governments in the New York area alone, and 20,000 throughout the United States. Most U.S. metropolitan areas have a **council of government**, consisting of representatives of the various local governments, and that can do some planning for the entire area. There are two kinds of metropolitan-wide governments. A **federation system** of government combines the various municipalities of a metropolitan area into a single government. Toronto, Ontario has a federation system. Some U.S. cities have consolidated city and county governments. Indianapolis and Miami are both examples of **consolidations**.

VII. Cities and Urban Land Use

A. Development and character of cities
4. Suburbanization and edge cities

C. Models of internal city structure
4. Changing employment mix
5. Changing demographic and social structures

D. Built environment and social space
1. Housing
2. Transportation and infrastructure
3. Political organization of urban areas
4. Urban planning and design

North American cities are increasingly following a structure that Harris calls the **peripheral model**. The peripheral model consists of an inner city surrounded by growing suburbs that combine residential and business areas and are tied together by a beltway or ring road. Nodes of business and consumer services called **edge cities** have developed around the beltway. Edge cities have grown from suburbs that were originally primarily residential.

In North American urban areas, the further one gets from the center of the city, there will be a decline in the density at which people live. This is called the **density gradient**. The number of houses per unit area of land will decline with distance from the center city. In North American and European cities in recent years, the density gradient has leveled out as more people have moved to the suburbs. **Suburban sprawl** has increased at the expense of agricultural land, and it results in the need for costly infrastructure. Several British cities are surrounded by **greenbelts**, or rings of open space, to prevent suburban sprawl. **Zoning ordinances**, which prevent the mixing of land uses, has resulted in segregated residential suburbs. Residents are separated from industrial and service activities, and poorer residents are excluded because of the cost, size, or location of housing. North American suburbs are no longer just areas of residential growth. Businesses have moved to the suburbs. Retailing has become concentrated in suburban malls. Factories and offices have also moved to suburbia. If they don't require face-to-face contact they can take advantage of the lower rents in the suburbs.

Several U.S. states are passing legislation and regulations called **smart growth;** it limits suburban sprawl and preserves farmland on the urban periphery. Maryland has done an especially good job in this area.

Suburban sprawl has resulted in an increased dependence on transportation, especially motor vehicles in the United States. Public transportation is much more important in most European and Japanese cities. Public transportation in the form of rapid transit is becoming more common in U.S. cities although it is still not recognized as a key utility that needs to be subsidized.

KEY TERMS

Annexation
Central Business District (CBD)
Central city
Census tract
City
Concentric zone model
Consolidated Metropolitan Statistical
Area (CMSA)
Consolidations
Council of government
Density gradient
Edge city
Federations
Filtering
Gentrification
Ghetto
Greenbelt
Islamic city
Latin American city
Megacity
Megalopolis

Metropolitan Statistical Area (MSA)
Micropolitan statistical area
Multiple nuclei model
Nodes
Peripheral model
Primary Metropolitan Statistical Area
(PMSA)
Public housing
Redlining
Sector model
Smart growth
Social area analysis
Sprawl
Squatter settlements
Underclass
Urban geography
Urbanization
Urbanized area
Urban renewal
Zone of transition
Zoning ordinance

Key Issues Revisited

1. Why do services cluster downtown?
-the central business district (CBD) contains a large percentage of a settlement's business services
-business services cluster downtown to facilitate face-to-face contact
-retailers with large thresholds or large ranges may also locate downtown

2. Where are people distributed within urban areas?
-the concentric zone, sector, and multiple-nuclei models help to explain where various groups of people live in urban areas
-these models provide a framework for understanding the distribution of social and economic groups within urban areas
-with modifications, the models also apply to cities in Europe and LDCs

3. Why do inner cities face distinctive challenges?
-inner-city residential areas have physical problems because of older, deteriorating houses

-inner-city residential areas have social problems as a result of a high percentage of low-income households
-inner-city residential areas have economic problems stemming from a gap between demand for services and supply of local tax revenue

4. Why do suburbs face distinctive challenges?
-the suburban lifestyle attracts many people
-transportation improvements, notably the railroad in the nineteenth century and the automobile in the twentieth century, have facilitated the sprawl of urban areas
-segregation and inefficiency are negative consequences of large-scale sprawl

Chapter 14: Resource Issues

A **resource** is a substance in the environment that is useful as well as feasible to access. Resources include water, soil, plants, animals, and minerals. This chapter deals with the two major misuses of resources, the depletion of scarce resources for energy production, and the destruction of resources through pollution. It then addresses the potential reuse and conservation of resources.

Key Issue 1 – Why are resources being depleted?

VI. Industrialization and Economic Development

A. Growth and diffusion of industrialization
1. The changing roles of energy and technology

Animate power is supplied by humans and animals. Since the Industrial Revolution there has been a tremendous increase in **inanimate power**, which is generated by machines. Three **fossil fuels**, oil, natural gas, and coal, provide five-sixths of the world's energy. In some LDCs **biomass fuel**, such as wood, plant material, and animal waste, is still the major source of fuel.

Fossil fuels are examples of **nonrenewable energy**. Remaining supplies are **proven reserves** and **potential reserves**. The world's proven reserves of natural gas will last for about 49 years, which is slightly more than petroleum reserves and much less than coal reserves. New technology can make potential reserves a reality but extraction is now much harder. New fields may yet be discovered, and unconventional sources may be developed.

Fossil fuels are unevenly distributed around the globe. China extracts 39% of the world's coal, and the United States extracts 16%. Australia, India, Russia, and South Africa also all have major reserves. Saudi Arabia, Iran, Iraq, Kuwait, and the United Arab Emirates, all of which are members of the **Organization of Petroleum Exporting Countries (OPEC)**, have 60 % of the world's oil reserves. Russia and the United States each account for one-fourth of world natural gas production. A few LDCs in Africa, Asia, and Latin America have extensive reserves of one or more fossil fuels, but most have little. MDCs currently consume about three-quarters of the world's energy although LDCs, especially China, are beginning to consume more as they become developed.

Nuclear power is becoming an increasing energy source, and it now supplies about one-sixth of the world's electricity. The world's leading generators of nuclear power are the United States, France, and Japan. A nuclear power plant produces electricity from energy released by splitting uranium atoms in a process called **fission**. Problems associated with nuclear power include potential accidents, **radioactive waste**, generation of plutonium, a limited uranium supply, geographic distribution, and cost. **Nuclear fusion** could address some of the issues associated with nuclear power. It fuses hydrogen atoms to form helium but can only occur at very high temperatures. Thus fusion has not yet been successfully used to generate power.

Minerals are plentiful on the Earth's surface and are potential resources if people can find a use for them. Minerals are either metallic or nonmetallic. Nonmetallic metals include various stones and sand, as well as nitrogen, phosphorus and other sources of fertilizer. Metallic minerals are ferrous, derived from iron, or **nonferrous** of which the most abundant is aluminum.

Key Issue 2 – Why are resources being polluted?

V. Agriculture and Rural Land Use

D. Modern commercial agriculture
4. Environmental impacts of agriculture

VI. Industrialization and Economic Development

B. Contemporary patterns and impacts of industrialization and development
5. Natural resources and environmental concerns

Air, water, and land remove and disperse waste, but **pollution** will occur when more waste is added than a resource can accommodate. **Air pollution** is a concentration of trace substances at a greater level than occurs in average air. The burning of fossil fuels generates most air pollution. Air pollution may contribute to global warming because of the **greenhouse effect**, which is when carbon dioxide traps some of the radiation emitted by the Earth's surface. The **ozone** layer of the Earth's atmosphere absorbs dangerous ultra violet (UV) rays from the Sun but is threatened by pollutants called **chlorofluorocarbons (CFCs).**

Pollution in the form of tiny droplets of sulfuric acid and nitric acid, formed as a result of the emission of burning fossil fuels, return to the Earth's surface as **acid deposition**. When dissolved in water, the acids may fall as **acid precipitation** which damages lakes and agricultural land in regions of heavy industrial development. Urban air pollution consists of carbon monoxide, hydrocarbons, and particulates. In the presence of sunlight this forms **photochemical smog** which is a serious problem in many urban areas.

Most water pollution is generated by water-using industries, municipal sewage, and agriculture. Polluted water can harm aquatic plants and animals. It also causes waterborne diseases such as cholera, typhoid, and dysentery, especially in LDCs that suffer from poor sanitation and untreated water.

Paper products constitute the largest percentage of solid waste in the United States. Most of this waste is disposed in **sanitary landfills**. The number of landfills in the United States has declined by three-fourths since 1990; there are now a smaller number of larger regional landfills. Incineration reduces the bulk of trash by about three-fourths, but burning releases toxins into the air. The disposal of hazardous waste is especially difficult. Hazardous waste sites, such as Love Canal, near Niagara Falls, New York, have leaked and caused health problems.

Key Issue 3 – Why are resources reusable?

VI. Industrialization and Economic Development

A. Growth and diffusion of industrialization
1. The changing roles of energy and technology

B. Contemporary patterns and impacts of industrialization and development
5. Natural resources and environmental concerns

The leading **renewable resources** are biomass and hydroelectric power. **Geothermal energy** and **wind power** are also becoming important. Wind energy is created by windmills in **wind farms**. Geothermal energy is generated from hot water or steam in volcanic areas, especially Iceland. Wood and plants are important forms of biomass that are renewable resources if they are carefully harvested. The energy of moving water has been used to generate **hydroelectric power**, which is the second-most important source of electricity after coal, supplying about one-fourth of the world's demand. The biggest drawback with hydroelectric power is that it is often generated by the building of dams that can cause serious environmental damage.

Solar energy is free and **ubiquitous**, and thus potentially the most important renewable resource. It can be harnessed either through passive or active means. **Passive solar energy systems** capture solar energy without any special devices whereas **active solar energy systems** collect solar energy and convert it to heat energy or electricity. In direct electric conversion, solar radiation is captured with **photovoltaic cells**, which convert light energy to electrical energy. **Recycling** is the separation, collection, processing, and reuse of unwanted material. Recycling has increased in the United States from 7% of all solid waste in 1970 to about 33% in 2007. Recycled products are picked up, processed, and manufactured into marketable products

Key Issue 4 – Why can resources be conserved?

VI. Industrialization and Economic Development

B. Contemporary patterns and impacts of industrialization and development
5. Natural resources and environmental concerns
6. Sustainable development

According to the United Nations, **sustainable development** is "development that meets the needs of the present without compromising the ability of future generations to meet their own needs." **Preservation** is the maintenance of resources in their present condition whereas **conservation** is the sustainable use and management of natural resources. Sustainable development advocates the limited use of renewable resources so that the environment can supply them indefinitely. Some critics, such as the World Wildlife Fund, argue that the world surpassed its sustainable level around 1980.

Closely related to sustainable development is **biodiversity**, which refers to the variety of plant and animal species across the Earth's surface or in a specific place. When biodiversity is protected, sustainable development is promoted. More than one-half of the Earth's species are located in tropical forests, and the main cause of high rates of species extinction is rapid deforestation.

KEY TERMS

Acid deposition
Acid precipitation
Active solar energy systems
Air pollution
Animate power
Biodiversity
Biomass fuel
Chlorofluorocarbon (CFC)
Conservation
Ferrous
Fossil fuels
Fission
Geothermal energy
Greenhouse effect
Hydroelectric power
Inanimate power
Nonferrous
Nonrenewable energy
Nuclear fusion
Nuclear power

Organization of Petroleum Exporting Countries (OPEC)
Ozone
Passive solar energy systems
Photochemical smog
Photovoltaic cells
Pollution
Potential reserve
Preservation
Proven reserve
Radioactive waste
Recycling
Renewable energy
Resource
Sanitary landfill
Sustainable development

Ubiquitous energy/resources
Wind farms
Wind power

Key Issues Revisited

1. Why are resources being depleted?
-consumption of resources results in depletion
-fossil fuels and mineral are distributed unevenly across the Earth's surface, and supplies are not found in places where demand is highest

2. Why are resources being polluted?
-people are damaging and destroying the Earth's resources through pollution
-pollution is the discharge of waste at a rate that exceeds the environment's capacity to absorb it
-pollutants are discharged into the atmosphere, water, and onto land

3. Why are resources reusable?

-depletion and destruction of scarce resources can be minimized by converting from nonrenewable to renewable sources of energy and by recycling more unwanted waste

4. Why can resources be conserved?

-sustainable development promotes economic development while not reducing the world's current resource base

-maintaining biodiversity through minimizing species extinction is critical to conserving natural resources

Activities

Activity 1: Geography: Its Nature and Perspectives

Geographers study the relationship between humans and the environment. When analyzing the spatial distributions of human settlements, they are looking for a global connection or pattern to understand this relationship. Think about the two theories of where humans live on Earth: Possibilism and Environmental Determinism to answer the following questions.

Look at the following map series: 1-14 (climate regions), 2-2 (World Population), 2-3 (Ecumene), 2-4 (Arithmetic Density) 2-5 and (Physiological Density).
1.   Is there a relationship between map 1-14 and 2-2?
2.   Now compare 1-14 and 2-3 for a historical look at human settlements. Is there a relationship between these maps?
3.   Compare 1-14 with 2-4; is there a relationship between population density and climate?
4.   Now compare 1-14 to 2-5, can you see a relationship there?
5.   If you glance at all map sets, what conclusion can you draw with the relationship between the environment and spatial patterns of settlement?
6.   With this evidence, does one theory hold true?

Possible Answers:
1. It appears that areas that are most populated are located in regions with humid tropical, semiarid, humid subtropical and humid continental climates. There is definitely a relationship with the map in the subarctic, ice cap and tundra climates, where people do not live.
2. Intensive settlement through out time has been located near coastlines and if rivers were present on these maps, you would notice that the settlement pattern is also near them.
3. The relationship between the arithmetic density map and the climate map does not seem to hold true compared to the choropleth dot map 2-2. The difference in this map projection is that on 2-4 it is obvious that in places like India with a high arithmetic density, if people were distributed uniformly across the landscape, people would be living in desert climates as well. The better comparison for where people live would be in comparing the first map sets which shows the location of the majority of people.
4. Physiological density is the number of people per unit area of arable land, so when we look at climate maps to compare, it appears that there is a relationship between the desert and the physiological density. As you think about it that makes sense, in the desert, one area of farmland would need to feed more people, therefore the density would be higher. So on this map; we see a direct correlation to climate regions.

5. Humans will live where the climate is fairly mild, and where they have easy access to the coast and fresh water. Landlocked countries on all of these map sets show that they are less likely to have large human settlements, as are areas with harsh climates. It is also obvious from this comparison that areas with large populations are not evenly distributed, even within a country (look at India and China). The global commonalities that affect where people live are: 2/3rds of the world live within 300 miles of the ocean, in low lying areas with fertile soil and temperate climates, in the northern hemisphere between 10-55 degrees latitude.

6. Environmental determinism (Humboldt and Ritter) explains the relationship between the physical environment and human actions. Possibilism says that the physical environment may limit some human actions but that people have the ability to adjust to their environment, so in fact both theories might hold true; however if you look only at the maps, Humboldt and Ritter's theory would hold because according to the maps, people are living in environments that are conducive to human actions (i.e. Farming). It would be difficult to prove, via the maps, Possibilism as there is not evidence supporting people living in extreme conditions, like the Arctic.

Activity 2: Population

When looking at population issues, geographers are interested in the question, "Is the world overpopulated?" As we study this issue, we look at many different criteria to find the answer.

1. Define in your own words the term "overpopulation," do you think the world is overpopulated? Why? Why not? Would Malthus agree with you? What about Esther Boserup?
2. Define the following terms: crude birth rate, crude death rate, rate of natural increase, total fertility rate, age cohort and dependency ratio.
3. Go on the internet to the site http://www.census.gov/ipc/www/idbpyr.html and analyze population pyramids for the following countries: China, India, Indonesia, and France. Create a table which compares and contrasts these pyramids.
4. What conclusions/predictions can you make about population growth in the four populated regions of the Earth that you obtained population pyramids for?

Possible Answers:

1. Overpopulation is the relationship between the total number of people on Earth and the availability of resources. Many population theorists, like Malthus, would say that because population growth exponentially and food supply grows arithmetically that eventually we will not be able to feed our people. Unlike Malthus, Esther Boserup believed that humans are unique creatures, who will be able, through technological advances in agriculture, to produce enough food to feed the masses.

2. Crude birth rate is the # of live persons per 1,000.
   Crude death rate is the # of deaths per 1,000.
   Total fertility rate is the # of women between the ages of 15-49.
   Rate of natural increase is the percentage by which population grows each year.
   Age cohort is the break down of a population by age, (i.e. 0-4 years old would be a cohort.
   Dependency ratio is the number of young and old people in a population who are not in the work force.

3.

COUNTRY	SIMILARITIES	DIFFERENCES
CHINA	•Shaped like France, •Evidence to support a population explosion around 1970 due to bulge in age cohort 30-35 in 2000, like in France too, •Women will out live men, •Population continues to be high because of the amount of people who were present when the government imposed population policies. It will take until 2050 to see an actual decline in the total population.	•Extremely high total population compared to Indonesia, and France, •India and Indonesia do not appear to have experienced a population explosion in any cohort (no baby boom)
INDIA	•India and Indonesia are both bell shaped, which supports a continuing population growth, •The population will continue to growth, as in Indonesia and will have fewer older people to support the young	•Unlike France and China, it does not appear that India's rate of natural increase is going to slow down in the next 50 years, •Similarly, India will continue to have a large majority of their population young and within the total fertility rate
INDONESIA	•Like India, the population pyramids are bell shaped, •Population is predicted to continue to grow for the next 50 years	•Unlike India or China, Indonesia's overall population is quite a bit smaller •Indonesia's population will begin to age in the next 50 years and the age cohorts age 65 will see great increases
FRANCE	•Population pyramids for France are similar to China, in that they are in a column shape, •Like China, France appears to have had a population explosion (baby boom) in the 1970's	•France has a low total population compared to all three other countries •By 2050 France will be the only country with people living longer than 100 years

4.   As population continues to stabilize in places like China and India, they will still experience population stresses, because of the total number of people in their populations. India and Indonesia will have a large number of children, who will need to be taken care of, (i.e. health care, education). France on the other hand will lower their youth and will increase their elderly. Who will take care of the very old? Who will pay into the National Healthcare system, since there are fewer workers?

Remember that many people can argue that the world is overpopulated or not, the theme that you should always look for is the spatial distribution of people on Earth. It can be possible that certain regions are overpopulated and cannot provide necessary resources for their people.

Activity 3: Cultural Patterns and Processes

Geographers are interested in the spatial distribution of culture. Remember that culture is like luggage, people carry it with them where ever they go (relocation diffusion). In this activity you are asked to analyze your cultural group, showing evidence from other places on Earth that has migrated to your neighborhood.

1. List the types of leisure activities people in your town are involved with.
2. What type of food is dominant in your cultural group?
3. What is the predominant type of housing present?
4. What language do most people speak? Are other languages spoken?
5. What religion dominates your cultural landscape?
6. What is the main ethnic group present in your town? Are others present? How can you tell?

By analyzing your answers to these questions, is their "An American Culture," or are we a melting pot of cultures?

Possible Answers:
(Note: answers will vary according to your geographic location)

1. In my town, most leisure activities revolve around sports. People go to watch our profession sports teams, basketball, soccer, baseball, lacrosse and football. They also participate in many sports, including water and snow skiing. Our cultural landscape reflects this, with the many sporting venues for the professional athletes.
2. I would say there are many types of food present. Our city has many ethnic resteraunt that reflect the many different types of people that live here. Overall, most people like steak and potatoes or McDonalds.
3. All of the housing looks the same in the suburbs, downtown; houses are very old and made of bricks.
4. Most people speak English as their predominant language; however other languages, like Spanish can be heard.
5. Christianity is the main religion. Many different denominations are present. You can see many types of churches as you drive down a main road; Protestant, Catholic, even Eastern Orthodox.
6. Most people living here are white. I know that there are also areas with different ethnic groups; Hispanic, Vietnamese, and Ethiopian all are present. I can tell this from the signs on buildings and streets (toponyms). Also the types of food and other services available reflect this.

It seems that there is an "American Culture" that is made up of blue jeans, fast cars and fast foods; and part of that culture has embedded within it a melting pot from all corners of the earth.

Activity 4: Political Organization of Space

In this unit, the focus has been on how boundaries are formed in the world. You looked at historical divisions with colonial boundaries being drawn that did not mesh with ethnic boundaries. In our contemporary world, since the fall of the Soviet Union and end of the Cold War, boundaries continue to be redefined. One of the ever present situations in Europe, as you have read, is the expansion of the European Union into Eastern Bloc countries.

This activity deals with the European Union granting Turkey membership. This membership has come with a barrage of criticism. If you were a voting member of the European Union how would you vote?

1. Go to the website http://en.wikipedia.org/wiki/European_Union
2. Complete the following chart regarding European Union membership.

Member Nations	
Governmental leaders	
Institutions and their geographic locations	
Candidate countries	

3. Does Turkey meet the criteria for joining? If so, what other issues come up when you were investigating their entrance into the EU?

4. How would you vote and why?

Possible Answers:
1.   Website access

2.

Member Nations	Belgium, France, West Germany, Italy, Luxembourg, Netherlands (1957), Denmark, Ireland, United Kingdom (1973), Greece (1981), Portugal, Spain (1986), East Germany after reunification (1990), Austria, Finland, Sweden (1995), Cyrus, Czech Republic, Estonia, Hungary, Latvia, Lithuania, Malta, Poland, Slovakia, Slovenia (2004), Bulgaria and Romania (2007).
Governmental leaders	EU Summit—Angela Merkel/Germany Council—Frank-Walter Steinmeier Commission—Jose Manuel Barroso Parliament—Hans-Gert Pottering
Institutions and their geographic locations	European Commission-Brussels, Belgium European Parliament-Strasbourg, Germany European Court of Justice-Luxembourg European Central Bank-Frankfurt, Germany
Candidate countries	Turkey, Croatia, Albania, Bosnia and Herzegovina, Montenegro and Serbia

3.   Turkey might eventually be able to meet the criteria, if they do the economic and social reforms that the European Union Charter calls for. However, significant issues will hamper their entry, the Cyprus dispute, issues about the Armenia Holocaust, possibly the fact that they have a Muslim majority and last, one of geography---is Turkey entirely in Europe? The original charter does not specify strict geographic criteria, but the EU Parliament continues to bring up the issue that Turkey lies both in Europe and Asia, so political geography comes into play. It is quite clear from all evidence that they will not be joining any time soon.

4.   ANSWERS WILL VARY.... Possible answer, yes, I would vote for them to join because as you look at the natural of a supranational organization like the European Union, the formation was to promote economic stability in the region and now possibly peace and security. If a country like Turkey is allowed to join, they will be able, due to their geographic location, help the EU obtain these goals.

Activity 5: Agricultural and Rural Land Use

As you learned in this unit, geographers try to find patterns across the landscape. If you've ever flown in an airplane, then you know that agricultural practices are quite evident on the landscape. In this activity, you will try to determine where the "typical" farmer in the world might be located and what type of agriculture practices they would use.

1.   Look at FIGURE 10-5 in your book. This map set compares climate regions with distinctive types of agricultural practices around the world. Based on your knowledge of agriculture, answer the following questions:
      A.   What type of farming occurs in dry regions of the world?
      B.   What type of farming is practiced in India?
      C.   What about China?
      D.   What is the predominant type of farming found in the Western part of the United States?
      E.   ‚What about the area east of the Mississippi River?
      F.   What type of farming is practiced in Western Europe?
      G.   What is the difference between farming in India and China with farming in the United States and Western Europe?

2.   Now look at FIGURE 2-2 (World Population).
      A.   Where are the most populated regions in the world?
      B.   What type of farming is practiced there?

3.   Based on your analysis, where are most agriculturalists located and what type of agriculture do they practice?

Possible Answers:
1.   A.   Dry regions have little or no agriculture and pastoral nomadism. There are, however, little pockets of commercial gardening present.
      B.   Indians practice intensive subsistence, wet rice dominant, wet rice not dominant, shifting cultivation and plantation.
      C.   The Chinese are similar to the Indians; however a large portion of Western Chinese practice pastoral nomadism.
      D.   Livestock ranching and some grain production.
      E.   East of the Mississippi River, the United States practices Dairy farming, mixed crop and livestock and grain production.
      F.   Western European nations practice Mediterranean agriculture, dairy and mixed crop and livestock agriculture.
      G.   India and China practice subsistence agriculture where as the United States and Western Europe practice commercial agriculture.
2.   A.   The most populated regions are in India and South East Asia.
      B.   The type of farming is subsistence agriculture.
3.   The "typical farmer" would be found in South Asia and would practice subsistence agriculture.

Activity 6: Industrialization and Economic Development

When geographers are looking at the issue of development, the issue of where are the more industrialized nations located? What about those nations that are living in poverty? Occasionally, when looking at the world in this way, we compare the world in two: the haves versus have nots.

1.   Look at the map on More or Less Developed regions of the world, FIGURE 9-8. This line is usually referred to as the Brandt Line, after Willy Brandt who wrote a report "The North/South Divide."

2.   Now look at FIGURE 9-1 (Human Development Index Map) and FIGURE 9-2 (Gross Domestic Product Map). Is there any correlation between FIGURE 9-8 and these maps? What can you conclude about the living standards of people who live above the line and below?

Possible Answers:

1.   Access to the map.
2.   The FIGURE 9-1 seems to be perfectly correlated with FIGURE 9-8. When I look at FIGURE 9-2, the correlation becomes even clearer. Regions to the North of the line have a high Human Development Index and higher per capita Gross Domestic Product than those to the South. From this information, I can conclude that industrialized, more developed (MDC's) nations are located to the North of the Brandt Line and less developed (LDC's) nations are to the South. A person living above the line would have a higher standard of living. They would live longer; have access to health care, clean water, sanitation, food, education, and consumer goods more often than those below the line. People would also work mainly in tertiary jobs that provide services in exchange for payment. Those living below the line would work mainly in primary jobs, and possible secondary ones. Their work, often times, would be for trade or barter, rather than by exchanging money. Women would be subservient and not participate in what little education there may be available.

Activity 7: Urbanization

1)   Identify and diagram the three models of urban structure that were discussed in Chapter 13.

2)   The United States Government has decided to award cities of over 2 million a grant to create a system of light rails (fast trains) that are run on energy generated entirely from renewable energy. Using your knowledge of these models, where would be the logical placement of the light rails in each? Why?

Multiple Choice Examination #1

1. A map is
A. a scale model of the real world
B. a very accurate model of the real world
C. an artistic fabrication of the real world
D. a method of scientific inquiry used to explain the real world
E. an ancient explanation of the cosmos

2. The purpose of Ptolemy's *Guide to Geography* was to
A. challenge the Catholic Church
B. support Isaac Newton's principles
C. to codify basic principles of mapmaking
D. to introduce the concept of geography information systems
E. to compliment the expansion of the Persian Empire

3. If Jim rented a car and wanted to drive from New York to Los Angeles he would be best advised to rent a car with _____, in order to reach Los Angeles in the most efficient way, going the shortest distance.
A. a GPS unit
B snow tires
C. a large luggage area
D. a GIS unit
E. a compass

4. An advantage of a Mercator projection map is
A. shape is distorted very little
B. landmasses at the poles are very accurate
C. it is very useful to display information across the oceans
D. the eastern and western hemispheres are separated
E. it was developed using GIS technology

5. The term *mash up* would most likely be used by
A. a GPS machine
B. GIS workers
C. Polynesian "stick chart" makers
D. a Robinson Projection map
E. Thomas Hutchinson in 1785

6. Because Japan is culturally homogeneous, geography would say it is an example of a
A. functional region
B. formal region
C. standard region
D. vernacular region
E. perceived region

7. Insurance companies look at maps with similar spatial distribution of cancer rates to determine whom to cover. This is known as:
A. spatial assimilation
B. economic bias
C. spatial grouping
D. spatial association
E. spatial discrimination

8. The idea that geographers should apply the law of natural science to understanding relationships between the physical environment and human actions was first describe by
A. Vladimir Koppen
B. Ellsworth Huntington
C. Alexander von Humboldt and Carl Ritter
D. Ellen Churchill Semple
D. Friedrich Ratze

9. The three main properties of distribution that geographers look at are
A. density, concentration, pattern
B. density, capacity, concentration
C. capacity, pattern, concentration
D. concentration, density, dispersement
E. concentration, capacity, pattern

10. In order to determine a country's farming efficiency, geographers would look at what type of density?
A. agricultural
B. physiological
C. arithmetic
D. concentration
E. clustered

11. The introduction of the euro allowed geographers to study what type of diffusion
A. contagious
B. expansion
C. relocation
D. hierarchical
E. stimulus

12. The gap in economic activity between the core and the periphery is known as:
A. economic colonialism
B. space time compression
C. distance decay
D. neocolonialism
E. uneven development

13. Chinese population clusters differ from those of Japan because
A. Japanese are concentrated in suburbs and Chinese are concentrated in urban areas.
B. Chinese are concentrated in suburbs and Japanese are in urban areas.
C. Japanese are concentrated in urban areas and Chinese are in rural areas.
D. Japanese are concentrated in rural areas and Chinese are in urban areas.
E. Japanese are concentrated in suburbs and Chinese are in rural areas.

14. The largest population cluster in the Western hemisphere is in the
A. Southwestern United States and Southeastern Canada
B. Southern United States and Northeastern Canada
C. Northeastern United States and Northeastern Canada
D. Northwestern United States and Northeastern Canada
E. Northeastern United States and Southeastern Canada

15. The most common measure of population change in a country is determined by looking at:
A. Crude birth rate, crude death rate and total fertility rate
B. Crude birth rate, total fertility rate and life expectancy
C. Crude birth rate, crude death rate and natural increase rate
D. Natural increase rate, life expectancy and infant mortality rate
E. Life expectancy, infant mortality rate and total fertility rate

16. Which revolution causes a country to move from Stage 1 to Stage 2 on the demographic transition model?
A. Medical Revolution
B. Agricultural Revolution
C. Industrial Revolution
D. Cultural Revolution
E. Organic Revolution

17. The dependency ration shows demographers
A. the number of males per hundred females in the total population
B. the number of people too young or too old to work
C. the number of babies born per 1,000 people
D. the number of children over 15 years old
E. the number of women between the ages of 15-49 years old

18. Which contemporary analyst believes that a large population could actually stimulate food production?
A. Garret Hardin
B. Ester Boserup
C. Thomas Malthus
D. Julian Simon
E. Paul Ehrlich

19. Why is Russia currently attracting many immigrants?
A. There is a stable government.
B. There are economic opportunities.
C. There is an abundance of farmland.
D. There are many natural resources.
E. None of the above.

20. Slavery and political instability are examples of what type of migration?
A. cultural
B. environmental
C. economic
D. educational
E. global

21. According to Wilbur Zelinsky's migration transition, international migration is more likely to occur in countries at what stage of the demographic transition model?
A. Stage 1
B. Stage 2
C. Stage 3
D. Stage 4
E. There is no correlation between migration and the demographic transition model

22. Which country houses the largest number of international migrants?
A. Germany
B. Russia
C. United Kingdom
D. France
E. United States

23. Most immigrants to the United States during the 1840-1850's came from
A. Ukraine and Romania
B. Austria and Czechoslovakia
C. Ireland and Germany
D. Vietnam and Laos
E. Sweden and Norway

24. Popular cultural is based on rapid simultaneous global connections made by
A. Television
B. Internet
C. High speed rail
D. Text messaging
E. All of the Above

25. Istanbul, Turkey has around 1,000 bostans which are run by many immigrants, their purpose is to
A. provides immigrants a place to live.
B. provides Turkey with a cultural experience.
C. provides small plots of land where a variety of vegetables can grow.
D. provide child care opportunities for immigrant's children.
E. provides micro lending opportunities to transnational corporations.

26. According to Jean Brunhes, the house is
A. a product of cultural tradition and natural conditions
B. a product of social class
C. a product of technological innovation
D. a product of architectural wonder
E. a product of human ingenuity

27. The northeast corner of a house is most sacred in
A. Java
B. Fiji
C. Laos
D. Madagascar
E. China

28. The three modes of folk forms of housing in the United States are
A. Southwestern, New England, Lower Chesapeake
B. New England, Middle Atlantic, Southwestern
C. Middle Atlantic, Lower Chesapeake, Southwestern
D. New England, Lower Chesapeake, Mid-Western
E. New England, Lower Chesapeake, Middle Atlantic

29. By using a thorough geographic analysis of human geography, we can ascertain that this state would have a relatively low rate of alcohol consumption
A. Nevada
B. Utah
C. Texas
D. California
E. New York

30. The official language in 56 countries is
A. Mandarin
B. French
C. Spanish
D. Swahili
E. English

31. Modern English is a co-mingling of
A. English spoken by the commoners and that of the Normans
B. Celtic language and common English
C. Celtic language and Norman language
D. the language of the Angles and that of the Jutes
E. the Language of the Saxons and that of the Angles

32. A map showing word usage boundaries uses _____ to illustrate where one word is most often used
A. contour lines
B. isoglosses
C. topographic lines
D. GIS layering
E. color coding

33. The Indo-European language family includes these branches
A. Indo-Iranian, Austro-Thai, Germanic
B. Indo-Iranian, Romance, Germanic
C. Indo-Iranian, Romance, Altaic
D. Indo-Iranian, Germanic, Benue-Congo
E. Indo-Iranian, Proto-Uralic, Germanic

34. Hottentots, a language using click clack sounds is part of the _____ language family
A. Khoisan
B. Nilo-Saharan
C. Niger-Congo
D. Afro-Asiatic
E. Altaic

35. The extinction of many languages once spoken in Peru is a result of
A. chain migration
B. relocation diffusion
C. political dominance and conversion
D. contagious diffusion
E. popular culture revival

36. Lingua Franca are most commonly diffused through
A. expansion diffusion
B. relocation diffusion
C. stimulus diffusion
D. contagious diffusion
E. commercial diffusion

37. A universalizing religion would seek to
A. appeal to one group of people
B. be located in one place
C. include people from other religions
D. appeal to all people
E. include only one cultural group

38. This group of Christians is clustered predominately north of Israel, in what is today called Lebanon
A. Maronites
B. Mormons
C. Coptics
D. Armenians
E. Ethiopians

39. Which country is comprised of a population that is 90% Shiite?
A. Iraq
B. Iran
C. Pakistan
D. Afghanistan
E. Oman

40. Mahayanist Buddhist are found primarily in
A. China, Japan and Korea
B. Tibet and Mongolia
C. Cambodia, Laos and Myanmar
D. Sri Lanka and Thailand
E. China and Tibet

41. The Baha'i religion was founded in 1844 in
A. Israel
B. Afghanistan
C. Pakistan
D. Iraq
E. Iran

42. Which universalizing religions find their roots in Judaism?
A. Christianity and Hinduism
B. Christianity and Buddhism
C. Christianity and Islam
D. Christianity and Sikhism
E. Christianity and Baha'ism

43. Muslims trace their origins through Abraham's son
A. Aaron
B. Saul
C. Solomon
D. Ishmael
E. Isaac

44. Baptists and Muslims are examples of
A. hierarchical religions
B. ethnic religions
C. animistic religions
D. autonomous religions
E. theocratic religions

45. Identity with a group who shares a biological trait is
A. race
B. ethnicity
C. nationality
D. multinationalism
E. self determination

46. The two most numerous ethnicities in the United States are
A. Hispanic Americans
B. African Americans
C. Asian Americans
D. American Indians
E. Both A & B

47. In which U.S. state would you find the greatest clustering of Asian Americans?
A. Hawaii
B. Mississippi
C. Texas
D. Maryland
E. Alabama

48. During the _____ Century, Africans experienced forced migration from Africa to America
A. 18th
B. First half of the 20th
C. 17th
D. Second half of the 20th
E. First decade of the 21st

49. The practice of _____ resulted when real estate agents convinced people to sell their homes at low prices
A. blockbusting
B. redlining
C. white flight
D. gerrymandering
E. desegregation

50. A country that is a very good example of a nation-sate is
A. Denmark
B. Russia
C. Yugoslavia
D. Czechoslovakia
E. France

51. Which is NOT an example of a centrifugal force?
A. ethnic cleansing
B. racial profiling
C. social classes
D. nationalism
E. indentured servitude

52. An example of an ethnic group divided among many countries would be
A. Croats
B. Serbians
C. Kurds
D. Turks
E. Druze

53. The first sovereign states that comprised a town and the surrounding countryside were known as a
A. nation-state
B. nation
C. country
D. colony
E. city-state

54. A territory that is legally tied to a sovereign state is called a
A. nation-state
B. nation
C. country
D. colony
E. city-state

55. The Caprivi Strip is an example of a _____ in a nation-state
A. elongation
B. fragmentation
C. proruption
D. perforation
E. fortification

56. In the 19th century the boundaries of Germany and Italy were aligned by
A. geometric lines
B. religious boundaries
C. ethnic boundaries
D. physical boundaries
E. language boundaries

57. Which of these states have a unitary system of government?
A. Rwanda
B. Russia
C. Canada
D. Brazil
E. India

58. The five permanent members of the United Nations Security Council include
A. China, France, Russia, United Kingdom, and United States
B. China, Spain, Russia, United Kingdom, and United States
C. China, Japan, Russia, United Kingdom and United States
D. China, Germany, Russia, United Kingdom and United States
E. China, Germany, France, United Kingdom and United States

59. Which organization is/was an example of a military alliance?
A. the European Union
B. the Warsaw Pact
C. the Organization of American States
D. the Commonwealth
E. the Organization of Petroleum Exporting Countries

60. The Human Development Index (HDI) includes which factors of development in order to judge a country's progress?
A. GDP, literacy rate, total fertility rate, educational level
B. GDP, life expectancy, total fertility rate, literacy rate
C. GDP, life expectancy, literacy rate, educational level
D. GDP, literacy rate, educational level, net emigration
E. GDP, life expectancy, educational level, net emigration

61. In what region of the world is the HDI significantly lower because females do not have access to educational opportunities?
A. Central Asia
B. Southwest Asia
C. Latin America
D. Southeast Asia
E. Oceania

62. India is an example of a country who
A. moved from the Self-Sufficiency development model to that of International trade
B. did not experience a traditional society in their past
C. has not incorporated modern technology into industries
D. is still at Stage 1 on the Demographic Transition Model
E. does not have a group of innovative elites to influence productivity

63. The main purpose of Fair Trade practices is
A. to make money
B. to provide cheap products
C. to protect workers
D. to create jobs
E. to protect the environment

64. The most "typical" human is a subsistent farmer living in which region of the world?
A. Oceania
B. Sub-Saharan Africa
C. North Africa
D. Latin America
E. Asia

65. Beans and cotton were first domesticated in which agricultural hearth?
A. Latin America
B. Africa
C. Central Asia
D. Europe
E. Southwest Asia

66. Shifting cultivation takes place mainly
A. in the tropics
B. at the poles
C. in arid regions
D. in rugged mountains
E. in the Mid-Western U.S.A.

67. One of the main characteristics of mixed crop and livestock farming is
A. the effort to grow crops is not uniform throughout the year
B. most crops grown are for human consumption
C. it is generally referred to as truck farming
D. crops are fed to animals rather than consumed by humans
E. the farm must be closer to the market because the products are highly perishable

68. In the von Thunen model of commercial farming, you would most likely find animal grazing in
A. the first ring
B. the second ring
C. the city center
D. the third ring
E. the outermost ring

69. Some commercial farms are converting to sustainable agriculture which is distinguished by
A. sensitive land management
B. better integration of crops and livestock
C. limited chemicals
D. ridge tillage
E. all of the above

70. The diffusion of ideas from the Industrial Revolution was slow, especially the railway system, because
A. people were waiting on patents
B. people would not share their inventions
C. there was not formal system to spread new technology
D. government policies forbid the sharing of technology
E. there was very little cooperation among the small, politically unstable countries of Europe

71. The location where transfer among different transportation modes is possible is called its
A. situation
B. single market point
C. break of bulk point
D. site
E. value added tax

72. Since most of the money in MDC's goes to both essential and nonessential consumer goods, we can look at which items to determine a society's development?
A. cars, telephones, health insurance
B. cars, telephones, child care
C. cars, telephones, televisions
D. cars, telephones, high speed transportation
E. cars, televisions, health insurance

73. If we were to map the percentage of the world that is an urban area, we would note a direct correlation to a map showing the percentage of workers in the
A. service industries
B. agricultural sector
C. mining industries
D. manufacturing industries
E. fishing industry

74. In the concentric zone model, most low income people would find affordable housing in
A. Zone 1
B. Zone 2
C. Zone 3
D. Zone 4
E. Zone 5

75. The process of limiting suburbs and preserving agricultural land is known as
A. redlining
B. smart growth
C. suburbanization
D. gentrification
E. sprawl

Free Response Questions for Multiple Choice Examination #1:

1. A. What is the difference between a state, a nation and a nation-state?

    _____

    _____

    _____

    _____

    _____

    B. Give an example of a failed nation-state with one reason why a nation state might fail.

    _____

    _____

    _____

    _____

    _____

2. According to Walter Christaller's Central Place Theory:

    A. Describe the optimal shape of a market and tell why it is the most efficient shape.

    _____

    _____

    _____

    _____

    _____

    B. Define the market area or hinterland.

    _____

    _____

    _____

C. Define range.

_____

_____

_____

D. Describe the threshold of services.

_____

_____

_____

_____

_____

_____

3.   A. Name two economic indicators that are useful in distinguishing between
        more developed and less developed countries.

_____

_____

_____

_____

_____

_____

     B. Define the tree sectors of economic activities and describe where (LDC vs.
        MDC) you would find most people employed in that sector.

_____

_____

_____

_____

_____

_____

Multiple Choice Examination #2

1. The earliest surviving map came from
A. Corsica
B. Sicily
C. Miletus
D. Alexandria
E. Shanghai

2. The revival of geography and mapmaking occurred during the
A. age of industrialization
B. age of the renaissance
C. age of enlightenment
D. age of reason
E. age of exploration

3. The type of distortion that can occur on a map of the world is/are:
A. shapes appear more elongated than they really are
B. distance between two points my become more increased or decreased
C. the relative size of areas might be altered
D. direction from one place to another can be distorted
E. all of the above

4. Much of the land in the United States was divided by
A. The Land Ordinance of 1785
B. The Homestead Act of 1862
C. The Louisiana Purchase 1803
D. Westward Expansion 1849
E. The Gadsden Purchase 1854

5. The four ways geographers use to identify a location on Earth are
A. place name, site, situation, toponym, grid coordinates
B. toponym, relative location, grid coordinates, place names
C. place name, site, situation, grid coordinates
D. grid coordinates postal address, site, and situation
E. postal address, grid coordinates, place name, site

6. The NFL Network is an example of
A. a formal region
B. a functional region
C. a vernacular region
D. a perceived region
E. a standard region

7. The cultural traits most often looked at in identifying a culture's location and global distribution are:
A. language, religion and ethnicity
B. language, religion and GNP
C. language, ethnicity and literacy rate
D. language, ethnicity and GNP
E. religion, ethnicity and literacy rate

8. In terms of geographic scale, globalization means:
A. the scale of the world is more isolated
B. the scale of the world is shrinking
C. the scale of the world is increasing
D. the scale of the world is status quo
E. None of the Above

9. In studying the Elk population in rocky Mountain National Park, geographers would be most interested in what type of density?
A. agricultural
B. physiological
C. arithmetic
D. concentration
E. clustered

10. The geometric arrangement of objects in space is known as
A. pattern
B. concentration
C. density
D. sustainability
E. dispersement

11. The spread of the Trojan virus among millions of computers around the world is a great example of what type of diffusion?
A. contagious
B. expansion
C. relocation
D. hierarchical
E. stimulus

12. Global patterns that are affected by population issues are concentrated in _____ and _____ where 2/3rds of the world's population lives.
A. Europe and Asia
B. Northwest Europe and South Asia
C. Southeast Asia and India
D. China and India
E. Europe and China

13. Southeast Asia's population are clustered
A. in Manilla
B. in Jakarta
C. on a series of islands
D. in urban areas
E. in suburban areas

14. Why are the lands located between the equator and 20 degrees North or South latitude inhospitable for humans to live in?
A. it is too cold there to live comfortably
B. the area is landlocked
C. there is a history of drought in the area
D. temperatures average over 100 F
E. it receives too much precipitation

15. Which demographic measure most affects the doubling time of a country
A. natural increase rate
B. total fertility rate
C. infant mortality rate
D. literacy rate
E. life expectancy

16. Which revolution pushed countries in Africa, Asia and Latin America to move into Stage 2 of the demographic transition model?
A. Medical Revolution
B. Agricultural Revolution
C. Industrial Revolution
D. Cultural Revolution
E. Organic Revolution

17. Which economist predicted that population was growing more rapidly than food supply?
A. Garret Hardin
B. Ester Boserup
C. Thomas Malthus
D. Julian Simon
E. Paul Ehrlich

18. According to E. G. Ravenstein, what is the most common reason people migrate?
A. cultural reasons
B. economic reasons
C. environmental reasons
D. chain migration
E. educational reasons

19. An intervening obstacle to migration would be
A. the Atlantic Ocean
B. the Pacific Ocean
C. the Rocky Mountains
D. the need for a passport
E. All of the Above

20. According to Wilbur Zelinsky's migration transition, internal migration occurs more often in countries at what sage of the demographic transition model?
A. Stage 1
B. Stage 2
C. Stage 3
D. Stage 4
E. Both Stage 3 and Stage 4 countries

21. Which regions have the largest percentage of net out-migration?
A. Asia, Oceania, Africa
B. Asia, Latin American, North America
C. Africa, Western Europe, Asia
D. Africa, Latin America, Asia
E. Oceania, Eastern Europe, Latin America

22. Most immigrants to the United States during the 1880's came from
A. Ukraine and Romania
B. Austria and Czechoslovakia
C. Ireland and Germany
D. Vietnam and Laos
E. Sweden and Norway

23. Amish folk cultural currently diffuses through with means?
A. international diffusion
B. interregional diffusion
C. hierarchical diffusion
D. contagious diffusion
E. stimulus diffusion

24. Why have bostans been present in Istanbul, Turkey for hundreds of years?
A. they provide immigrants a place to live.
B. they provide Turkey with a cultural experience.
C. they provide small plots of land where a variety of vegetables can grow.
D. they provide child care opportunities for immigrant's children.
E. they provide micro lending opportunities to transnational corporations.

25. Fred Kniffen considered the house to be a reflection of
A. cultural heritage
B. current fashion
C. functional needs
D. environmental impact
E. all of the above

26. The east wall of a house is considered most sacred in
A. Java
B. Fiji
C. Laos
D. Madagascar
E. China

27. By using a thorough geographic analysis of human geography, we can ascertain that this region of the United States would have a relatively low rate of alcohol consumption
A. northeast
B. north
C. south
D. southeast
E. northwest

28. The universal clothing symbol which has become a status symbol worldwide is/are
A. the poncho
B. blue jeans
C. the dashiki
D. the Mao jacket
E. the Aleut parka

29. Two billion people live in country where _____ is the official language
A. Mandarin
B. French
C. Spanish
D. Swahili
E. English

30. Why are geographers particularly interested in studying the differences in dialects?
A. they reflect distinctive features of the environments in which groups live
B. they are a reflection on how globalization works on folk cultures
C. they show how folk cultures affect popular culture
D. they predict what type of products can successfully be marketed in an area
E. None of the Above

31. _____ is determined by collecting data directly from people, particularly natives of rural areas.
A. contour lines
B. isoglosses
C. topographic lines
D. GIS layering
E. color coding

32. Estonia, Finland and Hungary speak the _____ language family, making theme the only European countries not to speak Indo-European
A. Altaic
B. Germanic
C. Romance
D. Uralic
E. Hamitic

33. The extinction of the Gothic language was a result of
A. chain migration
B. relocation diffusion
C. political dominance and conversion
D. contagious diffusion
E. popular culture revival

34. The official languages of the United Nations include all of the following EXCEPT:
A. Russian
B. Spanish
C. Urdu
D. English
E. Arabic

35. An ethnic religion would see to
A. appeal to one group of people
B. be located in one place
C. include people from other religions
D. include only one cultural group
E. All of the above

36. The three major branches of Christianity include
A. Roman Catholic, Coptic Church, Eastern Orthodox
B. Roman Catholic, Armenian, Protestant
C. Roman Catholic, Protestant, Latter Day Saints
D. Roman Catholic, Protestant, Eastern Orthodox
E. Roman Catholic, Protestant, Maronite

37. Approximately 50% of the world's Muslims live in what four countries OUTSIDE of the Middle East
A. Indonesia, Pakistan, Bangladesh and Malaysia
B. Indonesia, Pakistan, Sudan and Malaysia
C. Indonesia, Sudan, Malaysia, and India
D. Indonesia, Malaysia, India and Pakistan
E. Indonesia, Pakistan, Bangladesh and India

38. Tantrayanists Buddhist are found in
A. China, Japan and Korea
B. Tibet and Mongolia
C. Cambodia, Laos and Myanmar
D. Sri Lanka and Thailand
E. China and Tibet

39. The majority of Sikhs are located in the _____ region of India.
A. Punjab
B. Bangalore
C. Delhi
D. Ganges
E. Bengali

40. Daoism (Taoism) is an ethnic religion based on the teachings of
A. Buddha
B. Confucius
C. Meiji
D. Shakti
E. Lao Zi

41. Jews and Christians trace their origins through Abraham's son
A. Aaron
B. Saul
C. Solomon
D. Ishmael
E. Isaac

42. Roman Catholic and Mormon are examples of
A. hierarchical religions
B. ethnic religions
C. animistic religions
D. autonomous religions
E. theocratic religions

43. The single feature of a person's race that geographers are most concerned with is
A. eye color
B. hair color
C. blood type
D. skin color
E. body type

44. Identity with a group who share the cultural traditions of a particular hearth is
A. race
B. ethnicity
C. nationality
D. multinationalism
E. self determination

45. Geographers are most concerned with what geographic concept when they are studying they clustering of ethnicities
A. place
B. region
C. scale
D. density
E. space

46. In which U. S. State would you find the greatest clustering of Hispanic Americans?
A. Hawaii
B. Mississippi
C. Texas
D. Maryland
E. Alabama

47. African Americans migrated from the South to northern cities during the _____ century.
A. 18th
B. First half of the 20th
C. 17th
D. Second half of the 20th
E. First decade of the 21st

48. Identity with a group of people who share a legal attachment to a country is
A. race
B. ethnicity
C. nationality
D. multinationalism
E. self determination

49. A very important centripetal force for a nation-state is
A. ethnic cleansing
B. racial profiling
C. social classes
D. nationalism
E. indentured servitude

50. An example of a multinational state is
A. Wales
B. Scotland
C. Denmark
D. England
E. the Soviet Union

51. The dispute between the Sinhalese and the Tamils has occurred for more than 2,000 years in
A. Madagascar
B. Malaysia
C. Indonesia
D. Sri Lanka
E. Brunei

52. The smallest microstate recognized by the United Nations is
A. Malta
B. Liechtenstein
C. Palau
D. Singapore
E. Monaco

53. Political unity in the ancient world reached its height under the
A. Roman Empire
B. Greek Empire
C. Persian Empire
D. Mongolian Empire
E. British Empire

54. Which country shape could potentially suffer the most from isolation?
A. compact
B. prorupted
C. fragmented
D. elongated
E. perforated

55. The 49th parallel north of the equator is an example of what type of boundary?
A. geometric
B. religious
C. ethnic
D. physical
E. language

56. All of these states have a federal system of government EXCEPT
A. Rwanda
B. Russia
C. Canada
D. Brazil
E. India

57. The process of redrawing legislative boundaries is
A. blockbusting
B. redlining
C. segregation
D. desegregation
E. gerrymandering

58. Which country is NOT a member of the United Nation's Security Council?
A. Russia
B. China
C. United States
D. Spain
E. United Kingdom

59. Which organization seeks economic and cultural cooperation among former British colonies?
A. the European Union
B. the Warsaw Pact
C. the Organization of American States
D. the Commonwealth
E. the Organization of Petroleum Exporting Countries

60. According to the Human Development Index (HDI), the lowest ranking countries in the world would be found in which region?
A. Central Asia
B. sub-Saharan Africa
C. south Asia
D. Latin America
E. Southeast Asia

61. A major problem with Rostow's Development Model has been the
A. protection of inefficient businesses
B. need for a large bureaucracy
C. uneven distribution of resources
D. increase in dependency on LDC's
E. increase in the world financial market

62. A structural adjustment program would include
A. direct benefits to the poor
B. governmental reform
C. fiscal transparency
D. spending within a country's means
E. All of the above

63. One of the most fundamental differences between developed and less developed countries is best illustrated in
A. agricultural practices
B. medical programs
C. World Bank loans
D. fair trade practices
E. child care opportunities

64. The domestication of the largest number of animals used in agriculture occurred in
A. Latin America
B. Africa
C. Central Asia
D. Europe
E. Southwest Asia

65. Which five principal features distinguish commercial agriculture from subsistence agriculture?
A. purpose of farming, percentage of farmers in the labor force, use of machinery, farm size, agribusiness
B. purpose of farming, percentage of farmers in the labor force, use of machinery, farm size, slash and burn procedures
C. purpose of farming, percentage of farmers in the labor force, use of machinery, farm size, size of prime agricultural land
D. purpose of farming, percentage of farmers in the labor force, use of machinery, farm size, use of shifting agriculture
E. purpose of farming, percentage of farmers in the labor force, use of machinery, farm size, relationship of farming to other businesses

66. Pastoral Nomadism occurs
A. in the tropics
B. at the poles
C. in arid regions
D. in rugged mountains
E. in the mid-western U.S.A.

67. A characteristic of commercial gardening and fruit farming is
A. the effort to grow crops is not uniform throughout the year
B. most crops grown are for human consumption
C. it is generally referred to as truck farming
D. crops are fed to animals rather than consumed by humans
E. the farm must be closer to the market because the products are highly perishable

68. Von Thunen maintained that timber for construction and fuel would be found in
A. the first ring
B. the second ring
C. the city center
D. the third ring
E. the outermost ring

69. The _____ had the greatest impact on the industrial revolution
A. railroad system
B. textile industry
C. coal production
D. food processing industry
E. electric grid

70. The unique characteristics of a location like land, labor and capital are known as its
A. situation
B. single market point
C. break of bulk point
D. site
E. value added tax

71. A Post-Fordist strategy of production differs from that of a Fordist because
A. Post-Fordist are skilled workers who are encouraged to work in teams to achieve a common goal
B. Post-Fordist work in a large factory where laborers are skilled for only one task
C. Fordist are focused only on primary sector jobs
D. Fordist are skilled workers encouraged to work in tams to achieve a common goal
E. Post-Fordist are unskilled, cheap laborers

72. When geographers look at urban settlements, they often refer to a functional area with a county containing a city, where a large percentage of workers are employed as a
A. city
B. county seat
C. micropolitan area
D. metropolitan statistical area
E. census tract

73. While using the concentric zone model, you would find most commuters living in
A. Zone 1
B. Zone 2
C. Zone 3
D. Zone 4
E. Zone 5

74. The process of converting a low-income renter neighborhood into a middle-class owner neighborhood is
A. redlining
B. smart growth
C. suburbanization
D. gentrification
E. sprawl

75. According to the peripheral model, an inner city and the surrounding suburbs are tied together by
A. ring road
B. Interstate Highway
C. system of walking paths
D. a pedestrian crossing
E. a bus route

Free Response Questions for Multiple Choice Examination #2:

1.   A. Define and give an example of a language family, a language branch and a language group.

_____

_____

_____

_____

_____

_____

   B. Choose one language and describe how it diffused around the world.

_____

_____

_____

_____

_____

_____

_____

   C. What is a creolized language.

_____

_____

_____

2.   A. Define ethnic cleansing.

_____

_____

_____

_____

_____

_____

B. Choose one country that has experienced this and explain why it occurred.

_____

_____

_____

_____

_____

_____

3.   A. Why are commercial farmers converting to sustainable agriculture?

_____

_____

_____

_____

_____

B. Identify two of the three practices associated with sustainability and give an example of how a farmer would use each.

_____

_____

_____

_____

_____

_____

Free Response Questions- Unit II: Population

Using Figure 3-2, on page 82, answer the following questions:

A. Define the following terms as they are used in population geography.

a) Refugee

_____

_____

_____

b) Push and pull factors

_____

_____

_____

c) International and internal migration

_____

_____

_____

d) Voluntary and forced migration

_____

_____

_____

B. According to Figure 3-2, which countries have the highest number of internal refugees, and in which regions are the major flows of international refugees?

_____

_____

_____

_____

C. Explain the major push and pull factors for any one country on the map that has a large number of internal and/or international refugees.

_____

_____

_____

_____

_____

_____

_____

_____

_____

_____

Free Response Questions- Unit III: Cultural Patterns and Processes

Using Figure 8-10, on page 250, answer the following questions:

A. What is the difference between folk and popular culture? Give one specific example of each.

_____

_____

_____

_____

_____

_____

B. Identify and describe the types of diffusion associated with popular culture.

_____

_____

_____

_____

_____

C. Give two reasons why popular culture may cause problems, and illustrate each with a specific example.

_____

_____

_____

_____

_____

_____

Free-Response Questions- Unit IV: Political Organization of Space

A. Define the following terms as they are used in political geography.

a) Fragmented state

_____

_____

_____

b) Perforated state

_____

_____

_____

c) Prorupted state

_____

_____

_____

d) Superimposed boundary

_____

_____

_____

B. Name specific examples of fragmented, perforated and prorupted states from the map above, and explain why most of the boundaries shown on that map are examples of superimposed boundaries.

_____

_____

_____

_____

_____

_____

_____

_____

C. Give two principal reasons for the creation of proruptions in general, and give a specific reason for the creation of one of the proruptions shown on the map above.

_____

_____

_____

Free Response Questions- Unit V: Agriculture and Rural Land Use

With reference to Von Thunen's model of agricultural land use which is also known as *The Isolated State*, answer the following question. Use specific examples wherever appropriate.

A. Diagram the model and identify two assumptions made by Von Thunen that may not be true in reality.

_____

_____

_____

_____

B. According to the model what two costs must a farmer consider when deciding which crops to cultivate? What is the relationship between distance to market and land use?

_____

_____

_____

_____

_____

C. To what extent is the model relevant in more and less developed countries today?

_____

_____

_____

_____

Free Response Questions- Unit VI: Industrialization and Development

The Human Development Index (HDI), created by the United Nations, recognizes that a country's level of development is a function of economic, social, and demographic factors.

A. Within the economic factor of development, what categories of jobs does the HDI recognize, and how is the distribution of workers in these categories an indication of level of development?

_____

_____

_____

_____

_____

B. Identify three demographic indicators of development, and briefly explain how each can help to determine the level of development of a country.

_____

_____

_____

_____

_____

C. Select a specific country that has a very high HDI, and outline an economic, social, and demographic characteristic that helps to identify it as such.

_____

_____

_____

_____

_____

D. Select a specific country that has a low HDI, and outline an economic, social, and demographic characteristic that helps to identify it as such.

_____

_____

_____

_____

_____

_____

Free Response Questions- Unit VII: Cities and Urban Land Use

A. What is the difference between the primate city rule and the rank-size rule?

_____

_____

_____

_____

_____

B. Briefly discuss two reasons why London, New York, and Tokyo are considered the most important of the world cities.

_____

_____

_____

_____

_____

C. Briefly discuss two reasons why there is a much more rapid growth of cities in LDCs than in MDCs today.

_____

_____

_____

_____

_____

Answers to Multiple Choice Examination #1

1. **A.**
2. **C.** Ptolemy collected data from Roman soldiers to prepare maps, many of which were not improved upon for thousands of years.
3. **A.** Global Positioning Systems use satellites, tracking stations and receivers to pin point exact locations.
4. **A.** The biggest disadvantage of a Mercator Projection is that the higher latitudes appear much larger than they actually are.
5. **B.** The term refers to the practice of overlaying data.
6. **B.** Formal regions are also called uniform or homogenous regions.
7. **D.** See Figure 1-17. Spatial association identifies cultural, economic and environmental factors that display similar distributions.
8. **C.** Both were German geographers of the late 18th and early 19th century.
9. **A.**
10. **A.** agricultural density is the number of farmers per unit area of farmland.
11. **C.** See Figure 1-31.
12. **E.** this gap is best illustrated by the Brandt Line (30 degrees North) where wealthy countries are located north of the line.
13. **D.** Over half of the people in China live in rural areas, where as 40% of the Japanese live in 2 metropolitan areas, Tokyo and Osaka.
14. **E.** this cluster extends along the Atlantic Coast from Boston to Newport News, Virginia and westward along the Great Lakes to Chicago.
15. **C.**
16. **C.** New machines helped farmers to be more efficient, produce more food and thus freed people to work in factories.
17. **B.** this compares the number of people too young or too old to work with those in their productive years.
18. **B.** Boserup and Simon Kuznets believed that population growth generated more customers and more ideas from improving technology to produce more food.
19. **B.** See Case Study "Migrating from Uruguay to Russia."
20. **A.**
21. **B.** Internal migration is more important in countries at Stage 3 and 4.
22. **E.** About 3% of the world's population are international migrants.
23. **C.** Economic push factors and political instability forced these groups to migrate.
24. **E.** Popular culture is based on global connections through communication systems, transportation networks and other modern technology.
25. **C.** Bostan are small gardens.
26. **A.** Jean Brunhes is a French geographer.
27. **D.** The main door in Madagascar is on the west, which is considered the most important direction.
28. **E.** Fred Kniffen is an American cultural geographer who identified these hearths.
29. **B.** Because Latter-Day Saints (Mormons) are concentrated there.
30. **E.** Figure 5-1, this is more than any other language and is the predominate language in two more countries (Australia and the United States).
31. **A.** Modern English owes simpler words, like sky, horse, man to its Germanic roots

and more elaborate words, celestial, equestrian to the French invaders.

32. **B.** See Figure 5-8.

33. **B.** See Figure 5-9.

34. **A.** Refer to figure 5-19.

35. **C.** Peru once had 500 languages, but only has 57today, this is a direct result of missionaries work at converting indigenous people.

36. **A.** Expansion diffusion is the spread of a trait through a snowballing effect rather than the relocation of people.

37. **D.** A universalizing religion is global and seeks to appeal to all people regardless of culture or location.

38. **A.** this small Christian sect plays a disproportionately prominent role in politics in this region.

39. **B.** The majority of Muslims are Sunnis.

40. **A.** See Figure 6-4.

41. **E.** It grew out of the Babi faith founded by Siyyid 'Ali Muhammad known as the Bab.

42. **C.** Jesus was a Jew and Muhammad traced his ancestry to Abraham.

43. **D.** Where as Christians and Jews trace their origins through Isaac, Abraham's other son.

44. **D.** Autonomous religions are self-sufficient and interact among communities.

45. **A.**

46. **E.** Hispanic Americans make up 15% of the population and African Americans make up 13%.

47. **A.** Asian Americans make up 40% of the population of Hawaii.

48. **A.** At least 10 million Africans were forcibly brought to the Western Hemisphere.

49. **A.** this practice perpetuated white flight from the cities.

50. **A.** The territory is occupied by Danes who speak Danish and have strong sense of unity.

51. **D.** centrifugal forces break people apart, centripetal forces, like nationalism, bring them together

52. **C.** The Kurds are currently split mainly between Turkey, Iraq and Iran (see figure 7-19).

53. **E.**

54. **D.**

55. **C.** This 300 mile proruption disrupted communication among British colonies in South Africa and gave the Germans access to the Zambezi River.

56. **E.** These boundaries created states that were unified by a common language.

57. **A.** all of the other choices are federal states.

58. **A.**

59. **B.** The Warsaw Pact was the communist equivalent to NATO.

60. **C.** This index is used by the United Nations.

61. **B.** The level of literacy among females is the main reason the UN's HDI index is low in this petroleum rich region.

62. **A.**

63. **C.** Fair Trade means that products are made and traded to standards that protect workers and small businesses in LDC's.

64. **E.**

65. **A.** Mexico is considered to be the original hearth.

66. **A.** See figure 10-8, it is practiced by roughly 250 million people across 14 million miles.

67. **D.**

68. **E.** *The Isolated State* was written in 1826 to explain that commercial farmers compare the cost of land versus the cost of transportation when deciding what to grow and where to grow it.

69. **E.** This agricultural practice preserves and enhances environmental quality, see figure 10-25.

70. **E.** because cooperation could not be attained, some parts of Europe were delayed by 50 years compare to Britain.

71. **C.** important break of bulk points include seaports and airports.

72. **C.** geographers look at the amount of money spent on these as an indicator of development

73. **A.** in North America, 3/4th of workers are in service industries

74. **B.** Zone 2 is known as the zone of transition where industry and poor quality housing are found

75. **B.** most smart growth is due to legislation and regulation

Answers to Free Response Questions for Multiple ChoiceExamination #1

1. A. A **state** must include a delineated territory, must have a permanent population, must have a government and must have sovereignty. A **nation** is a homogeneous group of people who share the same culture, but do not necessarily have their own sovereign territory. A **nation-state** refers to a territory that is occupied by a particular ethnicity that has been transformed into a nationality.

B. An example of a failed nation-state would be Somalia, where the absence a significant, stable government has caused infighting among groups that share the same culture. (Other failed nation-states could include, Sudan, Ethiopia, Eritrea, Lebanon, Cambodia).

2. A. The optimal size of a market, according to Christaller, is a hexagon because the distance from the center is fairly uniform. If the area were a circle, they would need to overlap and squares cause great difference in the distance to the center.

B. The market area or hinterland is the area surrounding a service from which customers are attracted.

C. The range is the maximum distance that people are willing to travel for the service. Convenience stores have a very small range, where an NFL stadium has a much larger range.

D. The threshold of service is the minimum number of customers required to generate a profit.

3. A. The economic indicators that are useful in distinguishing between more developed and less developed countries are: 1. The economic structure of the country, 2. The workers productivity, 3. Access to raw materials and 4. The availability of consumer goods.

B. The three sectors of economic activity are:
--Primary sector jobs directly extracting materials from the earth like agriculture, mining and fishing. These jobs are found mainly in LDC's.
--Secondary sector jobs include manufacturing which processes, transforms and assembles raw materials. These jobs would be found in LDC's where an MDC has possibly outsourced jobs.
--Tertiary jobs are jobs that include goods and services in exchange for payment, like banking, education, insurance. These jobs are found in MDC's.

Answers to Multiple Choice Examination #2:

1. **C.** Miletus, in present day Turkey, was the center of geographic thought and mapmaking in the Ancient World.
2. **E.** Ptolemy's maps were rediscovered and translated into European languages.
3. **E.**
4. **A.** Land was divided into a system of townships that were 6 miles on each side. See figure 1-5.
5. **C.**
6. **B.** Functional regions are also called nodal regions because they are organized around one focal point or node.
7. **A.**
8. **B.** globalization is a force or process that involves the entire world.
9. **C.** arithmetic density is the total number of objects in an area.
10. **A.**
11. **A.** contagious diffusion occurs without regard for hierarchy or the relocation of people.
12. **A.**
13. **C.** The islands include Java, Sumatra, Borneo, Papua new Guinea and the Philippines.
14. **E.** the combination of rain and heat rapidly depletes nutrients from the soil and makes farming very difficult.
15. **A.** See figure 2-9.
16. **A.** medical transfers to these regions eliminated many of the traditional causes of death and enabled people to live longer.
17. **C.** "An Essay of the Principle of Population" was published in 1798.
18. **B.** push-pull factors generally influence a person's decision to migrate, they are push out of a country because of a bad economy, and pulled to another country with the promise of employment, for example.
19. **E.** obstacles historically were physical, like oceans, however contemporary obstacles include cultural issues like the need for a passport, VISA or Quota laws.
20. **E.** whereas international migration occurs most in Stage 2 countries.
21. **D.** this trend illustrates the pattern of migration from LDC's to MDC's.
22. **E.** the Industrial Revolution had diffused to these countries, causing rapid population increases and the loss of farmland.
23. **B.** recently many Amish have sold their farms in Lancaster, PA and moved to Christian and Todd County, KY because of the urban sprawl in Pennsylvania.
24. **C.** bostans are small gardens utilized by immigrants in Istanbul.
25. **E.** Fred Kniffen is an American cultural geographer.
26. **B.**
27. **D.** because Baptists, who generally consume very little, if any alcohol, are clustered there.
28. **B.**
29. **E.** see figure 5-2, 1/3rd of the world lives in a country where English is the official language.
30. **A.** the distribution of dialects is documented through the study of particular words and their usage.

31. **B.** see figure 5-8.

32. **D.** see figure 5-8. These languages originated in the Ural Mountains in present-day Russia.

33. **C.** many descendants of the Goths switched to speaking Latin when they converted to Christianity.

34. **C.** the official languages of the UN are Russian, Spanish, French, English, Mandarin and Arabic.

35. **E.** Ethnic religions appeal to one group, living in one place.

36. **D.** Universalizing religions are divided into branches, then denominations.

37. **E.**

38. **B.** see figure 6-4.

39. **A.** approximately 20 million Sikhs are clustered there.

40. **E.** Lao Zi (604-531? BC) was a contemporary of Confucius.

41. **E.** whereas Muslims trace their origins through his other son, Ishmael.

42. **A.** these religions have a well-defined geographic structure and organize their territory into local administrative units.

43. **D.** skin color is the fundamental basis by which people in many societies sort out where they reside, attend school and perform many daily activities.

44. **B.**

45. **C.**

46. **C.** Hispanic Americans are clustered in the southwest.

47. **B.** with the expansion of industries, like the auto industry, and the decline of sharecropping, many African Americans moved north between 1910-1920.

48. **C.**

49. **D.** centripetal forces bring people together, the other choices are all centrifugal forces which tear people apart.

50. **E.** the Soviet Union included 15 republics all with their own ethnic groups and also included many minor ethnic groups. See figure 7-17.

51. **D.** war between the two ethnicities erupted in 1983 and their situation remains very uncertain.

52. **E.**

53. **A.** the empire controlled most of Europe, North Asia and Southwest Asia.

54. **D.** a country like Chile or Italy has many areas isolated from the capital, like the far southern tips.

55. **A.** this "line on the map" was established in 1846 by a treaty between the United States and Great Britain.

56. **A.** Rwanda is a unitary state.

57. **E.** the purpose is to benefit the party in power.

58. **D.** all of the others, including France are permanent members of the Security Council.

59. **D.** this includes the United Kingdom and 52 other states that were once British colonies.

60. **B.** this index looks at GDP, life expectancy, literacy rate and educational level to determine a country's level of development.

61. **C.** petroleum rich countries increased because their commodity was in demand, whereas in some countries their main export might have actually decreased in price.

62. **E.** these programs seek to reform economic practices mainly in LDC's.

63. **A.** LDC's tend to comprise subsistent farmers and MDC's practice commercial farming.

64. **E.** these included cattle, goats, pigs and sheep, see figure 10-3.

65. **E.** see figure 10-5 and 10-6.

66. **C.** about 15 million people practice this, see figure 10-10.

67. **C.** Figure 10-23, truck comes from the middle English word meaning bartering or the exchange of commodities, truck farmers may sell their crops at a farmer's market, from the back of their trucks, or may sell to a large corporation.

68. **E.** *The Isolated State* was written in 1826 and explained that commercial farmers were most concerned with the cost of land versus the cost of transportation to markets, when deciding what and where to grow crops.

69. **A.** this system enabled factories to attract a large work force, bring in bulky raw materials and ship finished goods to markets, see figure 11-2.

70. **D.**

71. **A.** Post-Fordists focus on teams, problem solving and leveling (equality among management and workers).

72. **D.** there are currently 362 MSA's in the United States

73. **E.** this zone includes the suburbs, where high quality housing and good schools are located.

74. **D.**

75. **A.** this is sometimes called a beltway.

Answers to Free Response Questions for Multiple Choice Examination #2

1.   **A.** A **language family** is a collection of languages related through a common hearth or ancestor that existed long before there was a written record of its existence. A **language branch** is found within a family and are a collection of languages sharing the same ancestral language, but with fewer differences than the language family. A **language group** is a collection of languages within a branch. **An example would be: the Indo-European family is divided into 8 branches, one of which is Germanic and is broken down into the West Germanic group.**

        B. If we look at the diffusion of English around the world, we see that it has mainly diffused   through relocation, with early settlers coming to North America and bringing their language with   them. Also colonial practices of the British explain why a country like India or Australia might speak English, as well.

        C. A **creolized language** is a language that incorporated indigenous languages with that of   colonizer's language.

2.   **A. Ethnic Cleansing** is a process in which a more powerful ethnic group forcibly removes a less powerful one in order to create an ethnically homogeneous regions.

B. Rwanda would be an excellent example where ethnic cleansing has taken place. The Hutu tribe wanted to overthrow the Tutsi's and created a homogeneous country for the Hutus. Other good examples would be Cambodia, Bosnia, Kosovo and the Democratic Republic of the Congo.

3.   **A.** Commercial farmers are converting to sustainable agriculture in order to preserve and enhance their arable land.

    B. The three practices used in sustainable agriculture are: sensitive land management, which includes ridge tillage, the limited use of chemicals, where farmers learn to control weeds without chemicals, better integration of crops and livestock, allowing animals to consume the crops grown on the farm.

Answers for Free-Response Questions

Unit II: Population

A. a) Refugees are people who are forced to flee their homeland and who are afraid to return for fear of persecution because of race, religion, nationality, or political opinion.

b) Push factors make people move out of their present location. Push factors are economic, cultural, and environmental, and include war, famine, and political instability. Pull factors attract people to a new location, and they can also be economic, cultural, and environmental. People are often enticed to a new place because of a job.

c) International migration is the permanent movement of people from one country to another. Internal migration is the permanent movement of people within a country.

d) Voluntary migration is permanent migration done through choice, such as relocation for a new and better job. Forced migration on the other hand is not by choice but rather forced for cultural reasons, such as war and ethnic cleansing.

B. The countries with the largest number of internal refugees are Colombia, Sudan, Uganda, Rwanda, the Democratic Republic of the Congo, and Iraq. The major flows of international refugees are in central and eastern Africa, the Middle East, from Afghanistan and Myanmar to neighboring countries.

C. Sudan is an interesting example of both internal and international refugees, all due to war. As a result of the civil war, many people have been pushed out of Sudan to refugee camps in Uganda, Kenya, and Chad. Today, with the crisis in Darfur (western Sudan), many people are fleeing to other parts of Sudan as well as Chad.

Unit III: Cultural Patterns and Practices

A. Folk culture is practiced by a relatively homogeneous group, in a fairly isolated region, and is very slow to spread. The Amish culture is a good example. Popular culture is global and is spread throughout a heterogeneous group on a very large scale. It spreads quickly as a result of modern technology. Examples of popular culture are blue jeans and fast food restaurants.

B. Popular culture spreads through expansion diffusion which is a snowballing process. There are three types of expansion diffusion, all of which can be associated with popular culture. Hierarchical diffusion spreads from nodes of authority. Contagious diffusion is the rapid, widespread diffusion of an innovation through the population. Stimulus diffusion is the spread of an underlying principle even if the characteristic itself doesn't diffuse.

C. Popular culture may cause problems because an area loses its local diversity, such as giving up a native language to speak English. People may give up traditional values and adopt "western" ways of doing things. Popular culture is based on consumerism and material gain, and thus can pollute the environment through needless packaging or the building of a golf course in a desert.

Unit IV: Political Organization of Space

A. a) A fragmented state includes several separate pieces of land that are not together.

b) A perforated state has a hole in it; it completely surrounds another state(s).

c) A prorupted state is a compact state with an extension coming out from it.

d) Superimposed boundaries are created by powerful outsiders, such as the boundaries created by colonial powers.

B. Angola is an example of a fragmented state. South Africa is perforated, and Namibia is a prorupted state. All of these boundaries were imposed by European colonial powers.

C. A proruption can separate two countries that would otherwise share a boundary. Thus it can prevent adjacent boundaries between countries. Proruptions are also created to provide access to a resource such as water. The Caprivi Strip (which is now part of Namibia) gave German colonists access to the Zambezi River in southern Africa in territory that would otherwise have been part of Britain's African empire. It may have also contributed to the disruption of British communications in the region.

Unit V: Agriculture and Rural Land Use

A. Von Thunen's model of agricultural land use has a city at the center surrounded by a ring of horticulture and dairy farming. Outside that ring is one of forestry which in turn is surrounded by one of crop rotation, and agriculture that becomes more extensive the further one goes from the city. The ring that is furthest from the city is one of grazing. The model assumes that this is a uniform plain with no variation in physical geography. Von Thunen also assumed that there is equal ease of transportation in all directions.

B. A farmer must consider the cost of land, and the cost of transporting products to market. The relationship between distance to market and land use is critical because the cost of transporting each product is different. A farmer might choose a crop that does not yield as much profit per acre because transportation costs for the product are cheaper.

C. Even though the land use pattern around a city in the developed world no longer looks like this, the underlying principles are still the same. For example agricultural land use will always be more intensive closer to the market and more extensive the further one gets from a city. The cost of land and the cost of transporting goods to market are still critical.

The agricultural land use pattern around many cities in the developing world may still closely resemble the model. These regions do not have modern technology, such as refrigerated dairy containers, so the dairy ring must remain close to the city. Wood is a major building and fuel supplier in many of these countries. The land use pattern around Addis Ababa, Ethiopia is much the same as Von Thunen's original model.

In both the developed and developing worlds, explanations of the differences between reality and the model will enhance one's understanding of agricultural land use.

Unit VII: Cities and Urban Land Use

A. According to the primate city rule, the largest city in a country has twice as many people as the second-largest city. Moscow is a primate city in Russia because it is twice as large as St. Petersburg. The rank-size rule explains the pattern of settlements in a country where the *n*th largest settlement is 1/nth the population of the largest settlement. The relative size of settlements in Brazil and the United States follow the rank-size rule more than the primate city rule. Neither of these countries have one primate city although the extent to which they follow the rank-size rule is still difficult to determine from the map.

B. London, New York, and Tokyo are the most important of the world cities because they are much larger and more important than any other cities in their respective regions. All three are home to the world's most important stock exchanges. They all also contain larger concentrations of financial and business services than other cities in the world.

C. Population growth is much more rapid in LDCs than MDCs today. Cities are also growing much faster in LDCs. Much of this is the result of push factors in rural areas. Agriculture is collapsing in many developing regions and people are moving to urban areas in search of work. This is particularly true in Latin America where slums are growing on the outskirts of major metropolitan areas.

The migration trend in MDCs for the last few decades has been from urban to suburban areas. Edge cities have been created on the suburban fringe of many North American cities. Counterurbanization, or the movement from urban to rural communities, has been a growing trend in the last decade in the more developed world.

Unit VI: Industrialization and Development

A. The HDI recognizes jobs in the primary, secondary, and tertiary sectors of the economy. As a country becomes more developed, the percentage of workers in the primary sector will decline as the percentage in the secondary sector increases. Today more developed countries have the largest percentage of workers in the tertiary sector of the economy. The percentage of workers in agriculture is more than 60% in less developed countries, and less than 5% in more developed countries.

B. In more developed countries (MDCs), life expectancy is higher because people have better access to health care. The infant mortality rate is also much higher in less developed countries for the same reasons. The rate of natural increase is higher in less developed countries which puts a great strain on their resources. Cultural practices and a lack of education with regard to birth control contribute to such high rates of natural increase, especially in Sub Saharan Africa.

C. Japan has a very high HDI. The majority of people in this country work in the tertiary sector of the economy. Japanese people are generally very educated, and have access to quality health care. Life expectancy is around 80 years.
Afghanistan has a very low HDI. The people in this country work in the primary sector of the economy as farmers or pastoral nomads. Most Afghans to do have access to education; literacy rates are very low. They have a low life expectancy, and a high crude birth rate.